AGRICULTURE ISSUES AND POLICIES

UNITED STATES AGRICULTURAL TRADE

AGRICULTURE ISSUES AND POLICIES

Additional books in this series can be found on Nova's website under the Series tab.

Additional E-books in this series can be found on Nova's website under the E-books tab.

AGRICULTURE ISSUES AND POLICIES

UNITED STATES AGRICULTURAL TRADE

TYLER E. BROOKS
AND
EMILY M. SANDERS
EDITORS

Nova Science Publishers, Inc.
New York

Copyright © 2011 by Nova Science Publishers, Inc.

All rights reserved. No part of this book may be reproduced, stored in a retrieval system or transmitted in any form or by any means: electronic, electrostatic, magnetic, tape, mechanical photocopying, recording or otherwise without the written permission of the Publisher.

For permission to use material from this book please contact us:
Telephone 631-231-7269; Fax 631-231-8175
Web Site: http://www.novapublishers.com

NOTICE TO THE READER

The Publisher has taken reasonable care in the preparation of this book, but makes no expressed or implied warranty of any kind and assumes no responsibility for any errors or omissions. No liability is assumed for incidental or consequential damages in connection with or arising out of information contained in this book. The Publisher shall not be liable for any special, consequential, or exemplary damages resulting, in whole or in part, from the readers' use of, or reliance upon, this material. Any parts of this book based on government reports are so indicated and copyright is claimed for those parts to the extent applicable to compilations of such works.

Independent verification should be sought for any data, advice or recommendations contained in this book. In addition, no responsibility is assumed by the publisher for any injury and/or damage to persons or property arising from any methods, products, instructions, ideas or otherwise contained in this publication.

This publication is designed to provide accurate and authoritative information with regard to the subject matter covered herein. It is sold with the clear understanding that the Publisher is not engaged in rendering legal or any other professional services. If legal or any other expert assistance is required, the services of a competent person should be sought. FROM A DECLARATION OF PARTICIPANTS JOINTLY ADOPTED BY A COMMITTEE OF THE AMERICAN BAR ASSOCIATION AND A COMMITTEE OF PUBLISHERS.

Additional color graphics may be available in the e-book version of this book.

LIBRARY OF CONGRESS CATALOGING-IN-PUBLICATION DATA

United States agricultural trade / editors: Tyler E. Brooks and Emily M. Sanders.
    p. cm. -- (Agriculture issues and policies series)
 Includes bibliographical references and index.
 ISBN 978-1-61209-128-0 (hardcover : alk. paper)
 1. Produce trade--United States. 2. Farm produce--United States--Marketing. 3. Exports--United States. 4. Agriculture--Economic aspects--United States. I. Brooks, Tyler E. II. Sanders, Emily M. III. Series: Agriculture issues and policies series.
 HD9005.U564 2011
 382'.410973--dc22
                      2010047106

Published by Nova Science Publishers, Inc. ✦ New York

CONTENTS

Preface		vii
Chapter 1	U.S. Agricultural Trade: Trends, Composition, Direction, and Policy *Charles E. Hanrahan, Carol Canada and Beverly A. Banks*	1
Chapter 2	U.S. Agricultural Trade Boosts Overall Economy *William Edmondson*	43
Chapter 3	Global Growth, Macroeconomic Change, and U.S. Agricultural Trade *Mark Gehlhar, Erik Dohlman, Nora Brooks, Alberto Jerardo and Thomas Vollrath*	59
Chapter Sources		105
Index		107

PREFACE

U.S. agricultural trade generates employment, income and purchasing power in both the farm and nonfarm sectors. This new book examines past trends and emerging developments by spotlighting the role of two specific factors that help steer U.S. agricultural trade patterns: global growth and shifts in foreign economic activity that affect U.S. exports and macroeconomic factors underlying the growth of U.S. imports

Chapter 1- U.S. agricultural exports for FY2010 are forecast by the U.S. Department of Agriculture to reach $100 billion, while agricultural imports are expected to reach $77.5 billion. The agricultural trade surplus is projected to be $22.5 billion. Exports of high-value products (e.g., fruits, vegetables, meats, wine and beer) have increased since the early 1 990s and now account for 60% of total U.S. agricultural exports. Exports of bulk commodities (e.g., soybeans, wheat, and feed grains) remain significant.

Chapter 2- U.S. agricultural trade generates employment, income, and purchasing power in both the farm and nonfarm sectors. Each farm export dollar earned stimulated another $1.65 in business activity in calendar year 2006. The $71.0 billion of agricultural exports in 2006 produced an additional $117.2 billion in economic activity for a total economic output of $188.2 billion. Agricultural exports also generated 841,000 full-time civilian jobs, which include 482,000 jobs in the nonfarm sector. Farmers' purchases of fuel, fertilizer, and other inputs to produce commodities for export spurred economic activity in the manufacturing, trade, and transportation sectors.

Chapter 3- After a decade of uneven export growth and rapidly growing imports, U.S. agriculture has begun to reassert its position in global trade markets. Rising exports and signs of moderating demand for imports mark a departure from previous trends. This report places past trends and emerging developments in perspective by spotlighting the role of two specific factors that help steer U.S. agricultural trade patterns: global growth and shifts in foreign economic activity that affect U.S. exports, and macroeconomic factors underlying the growth of U.S. imports. Consistent with actual changes in the level and destination of U.S. exports, model simulations corroborate the contention that renewed export growth can be sustained by expanding incomes and growing food import demand in emerging economies. In contrast, the rapid growth of U.S. agricultural imports appears less related to domestic income growth than to changing consumer preferences and other, perhaps less sustainable, macroeconomic conditions that fostered the growth of U.S. current account deficits.

In: United States Agricultural Trade
Eds: T. E. Brooks and E. M. Sanders

ISBN: 978-1-61209-128-0
© 2011 Nova Science Publishers, Inc.

Chapter 1

U.S. AGRICULTURAL TRADE: TRENDS, COMPOSITION, DIRECTION, AND POLICY

Charles E. Hanrahan, Carol Canada and Beverly A. Banks

SUMMARY

U.S. agricultural exports for FY2010 are forecast by the U.S. Department of Agriculture to reach $100 billion, while agricultural imports are expected to reach $77.5 billion. The agricultural trade surplus is projected to be $22.5 billion. Exports of high-value products (e.g., fruits, vegetables, meats, wine and beer) have increased since the early 1 990s and now account for 60% of total U.S. agricultural exports. Exports of bulk commodities (e.g., soybeans, wheat, and feed grains) remain significant.

Leading markets for U.S. agricultural exports are Canada, Mexico, China, Japan, the European Union (EU), South Korea, and Taiwan. The United States in 2010 is forecast to be the world's leading exporter of corn, wheat, soybeans, and cotton. The U.S. share of world beef exports, which declined after the 2003 discovery of a case of "mad cow disease" in the United States, is recovering as more countries have re-opened their markets to U.S. product. The United States, European Union, Australia, and New Zealand are dominant suppliers of dairy products in global agricultural trade. New Zealand and the United States are the main suppliers of nonfat dry milk to world markets, while the EU is the leading supplier of cheeses.

Among the fastest-growing markets for U.S. agricultural exports are Canada and Mexico, both partners with the United States in the North American Free Trade Agreement (NAFTA). U.S. agricultural exports to China, a member of the World Trade Organization since 2001, have grown at an annual rate of 15.7% since 1992.

Most U.S. agricultural imports are high-value products, including fruits, nuts, vegetables, wine, and beer. The biggest import suppliers are the EU and NAFTA partners, Canada and Mexico, which together provide 42% of total U.S. agricultural imports. Brazil, Australia, Indonesia, New Zealand, and Colombia are also important suppliers of agricultural imports to the United States.

According to estimates by the Organization for Economic Cooperation and Development (OECD), the United States provides the third-lowest amount of government policy-generated support to its agricultural sector among OECD countries. The United States' average applied tariff for agricultural products is estimated by the World Trade Organization to be 8.9%, a little more than twice the average applied tariff for non-agricultural products. Export subsidies, export credit guarantees, and market development programs are among the programs available to the United States to promote U.S. agricultural exports.

U.S. AGRICULTURAL EXPORTS, IMPORTS, AND TRADE BALANCE

- According to USDA, FY2010 agricultural exports are forecast to be $100 billion, well below the fiscal 2008 record, but the second-highest ever. Increased demand for both high-value products and commodities as the global economy recovers from recession is the main factor behind the FY2010 export number.
- U.S. agricultural imports are forecast to reach $77.5 billion in FY2010, a $4.1 billion increase over FY2009 agricultural imports.
- The $22.5 billion U.S. agricultural trade surplus forecast for FY2010 is well below FY2008's all-time high of $36 billion.

Table 1. U.S. Agricultural Exports and Imports, FY1988-FY2010F ($ billion)

Year	Exports	Imports	Balance
1988	35.3	21.0	14.3
1989	39.6	21.5	18.1
1990	40.2	22.6	17.7
1991	37.6	22.6	15.0
1992	42.4	24.3	18.1
1993	42.6	24.4	18.1
1994	43.9	26.6	17.3
1995	54.6	29.9	24.7
1996	59.8	32.6	27.2
1997	57.3	35.8	21.5
1998	53.6	36.8	16.8
1999	49.1	37.3	11.8
2000	50.7	38.9	11.9
2001	52.7	39.0	13.7
2002	53.3	41.0	12.3
2003	56.0	45.7	10.3
2004	62.4	52.7	9.7
2005	62.5	57.7	4.8
2006	68.6	64.0	4.6
2007	82.2	70.1	12.1
2008	115.3	79.3	36.0
2009	96.6	73.4	23.2
2010F	100.0	77.5	22.5

Source: U.S. Department of Agriculture. Economic Research Service, Outlook for U.S. Agricultural Trade, AES65, February 18, 2010, available at http://usda.mannlib.cornell.edu/usda/current/AES/AES-02-18-2010.pdf.

Note: F= Forecast.

SHARES OF U.S. CROP PRODUCTION EXPORTED: SELECTED COMMODITIES

- USDA estimates that production from one-third of harvested acreage is exported.

- In 2009/2010, a forecast 41.4% of the U.S. wheat crop will be exported, while 16.5% of the U.S. corn crop will move into world markets.
- The export share of soybeans is forecast to be 40.2% in 2009/2010. A decline from the previous marketing year is due in part to weakened foreign demand for meats and livestock feed.
- Cotton's export share in 2009/2010 is forecast to reach 80%, making cotton the United States' most export-dependent crop.

Table 2. U.S. Agricultural Exports: Shares of U.S. Crop Production Exported, 1990/1991-2009/2010F (percent)

Year	Wheat	Corn	Cotton	Soybeans
1990/1991	38.4	21.8	50.2	28.9
1991/1992	65.5	21.2	37.7	34.4
1992/1993	55.5	17.6	32.0	35.2
1993/1994	50.8	21.0	42.5	31.5
1994/1995	51.5	21.7	47.8	33.4
1995/1996	56.9	30.1	42.8	39.1
1996/1997	44.0	19.5	36.2	37.2
1997/1998	41.9	16.3	39.9	32.5
1998/1999	41.8	20.3	30.9	29.4
1999/2000	47.1	20.5	39.8	36.7
2000/2001	46.2	19.6	39.2	36.1
2001/2002	49.6	20.0	54.1	36.8
2002/2003	52.2	17.7	69.1	37.9
2003/2004	50.6	18.8	75.3	36.1
2004/2005	48.6	15.4	62.1	35.1
2005/2006	47.6	19.2	73.5	30.6
2006/2007	50.9	20.2	60.3	34.9
2007/2008	61.5	18.7	71.1	43.3
2008/2009	40.1	15.4	103.6	43.1
2009/2010F	41.4	16.5	80.8	40.2

Source: Calculated by CRS using data from the U.S. Department of Agriculture's Foreign Agricultural Service Production, Supply and Distribution Online database, http://www.fas.usda.gov/psdonline/psdHome.aspx.
Note: F = Forecast.

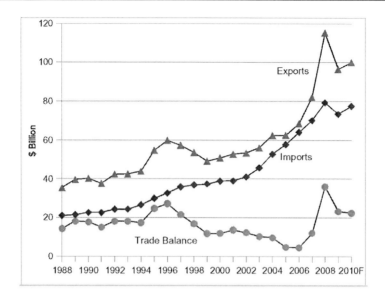

Source: U.S. Department of Agriculture. Economic Research Service. F = Forecast

Figure 1. U.S. Agricultural Exports, Imports, and the Trade Balance, FY 998-FY2010F

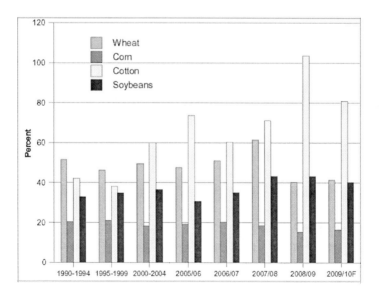

Source: U.S. Department of Agriculture. Economic Research Service.

Figure 2. U.S. Agricultural Exports: Share of U.S. Production Exported, 1990/1991-2009/2010F

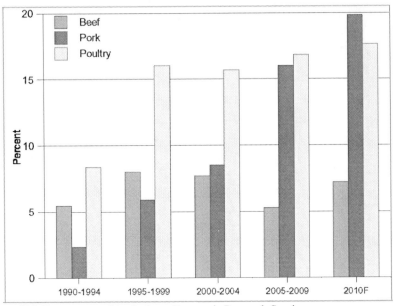

Source: U.S. Department of Agriculture. Economic Research Service.

Figure 3. U.S. Agricultural Exports: Shares of U.S. Production of Livestock Exported, 1990-2010F

SHARES OF U.S. LIVESTOCK PRODUCTION EXPORTED: SELECTED COMMODITIES

- U.S. livestock products are much less export-dependent than crops.
- Beef exports, which grew from around 4% of production in 1990 to almost 10% in 2003, have slowly recovered from export bans on U.S. beef following the 2003 discovery of a BSE-infected cow in the United States. The beef export share of production in 2010 is forecast to be 7.2%.
- Pork exports as a share of production have grown substantially, from less than 1.6% in 1990 to a forecast 19.8% in 2010.
- Poultry's export share of production has almost tripled since 1990, from 6.2% to a forecast 17.6% in 2010.

Table 3. U.S. Agricultural Exports: Shares of U.S. Production of Livestock Exported, 1990-2010F (percent)

Year	Beef	Pork	Poultry
1990	4.4	1.6	6.2
1991	5.1	1.8	6.4
1992	5.7	2.4	7.1
1993	5.5	2.6	8.9
1994	6.5	3.1	12.1
1995	7.1	4.4	15.7
1996	7.2	5.7	16.9
1997	8.3	6.0	16.3
1998	8.3	6.5	15.8
1999	9.0	6.6	15.6
2000	9.1	6.8	16.3
2001	8.6	8.0	18.0
2002	8.9	8.2	15.1
2003	9.5	8.6	15.2
2004	1.9	10.6	14.2
2005	2.8	12.9	14.9
2006	4.3	14.2	14.8
2007	5.4	14.3	16.5
2008	7.0	20.0	19.1
2009	6.6	18.1	18.8
2010F	7.2	19.8	17.6

Source: Calculated by CRS using data from the U.S. Department of Agriculture's Foreign Agricultural Service Production, Supply and Distribution Online database, http://www.fas.usda.gov/psdonline/psdHome.aspx.
Note: F = Forecast.

COMPOSITION OF U.S. AGRICULTURAL EXPORTS: MAJOR COMMODITY COMPONENTS

- The United States exports a wide range of agricultural products, including horticultural products, field crops, livestock products, and poultry.

- Oilseeds (mainly soybeans) and oilseed products (mainly meal and oil)—with a forecast value of $23 billion in FY2010—are the largest commodity component of U.S. agricultural exports.
- Horticultural product exports (fruits, vegetables, tree nuts, and their preparations)—forecast to be $21.5 billion in FY2010—comprise the second- largest commodity category of U.S. agricultural exports in FY20 10.
- Livestock and poultry products together would amount to more than $17 billion in FY2010.
- Field crop exports (feed grains, wheat, cotton, and tobacco) are forecast to account for $20 billion of U.S. agricultural exports in FY2010.

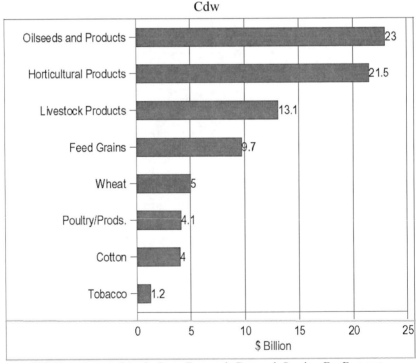

Source: U.S. Department of Agriculture. Economic Research Service. F = Forecast

Figure 4. U.S. Agricultural Exports of Major Commodities, FY2010F

Table 4. U.S. Agricultural Exports of Major Commodities, FY2010F ($ billions)

Commodity	FY2010F Exports
Oilseeds and Products	23.0
Horticultural Products	21.5
Livestock Products	13.1
Feed Grains	9.7
Wheat	5.0
Poultry/Prods.	4.1
Cotton	4.0
Tobacco	1.2

Source: U.S. Department of Agriculture. Economic Research Service, Outlook for U.S. Agricultural Trade AES65, February 18, 2010, available at http://usda.mannlib.cornell.edu/usda/current/AES/AES-02-18-2010.pdf.
Note: F = Forecast.

COMPOSITION OF U.S. AGRICULTURAL EXPORTS: BULK, CONSUMER-READY, AND INTERMEDIATE PRODUCT EXPORTS

- *Bulk agricultural exports* include products like wheat, coarse grains, cotton, and soybeans.
- *Intermediate products* have been processed to some extent and include products like wheat flour, soybean oil, and feeds.
- *Consumer-ready products* include both processed products such as breakfast cereals and products such as fresh fruits and vegetables.
- Until 1990, bulk agricultural exports were the mainstay of U.S. farm export trade. The total of high-value (intermediate and consumer-ready) products has exceeded the value of bulk agricultural exports in every fiscal year since FY1991.
- In FY2009, high-value exports accounted for 60% of total U.S. agricultural exports and bulk exports for 40%.

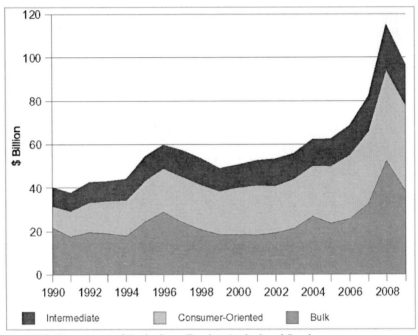

Source: U.S. Department of Agriculture. Foreign Agricultural Service.

Figure 5. U.S. Agricultural Exports, FY1990-FY2009: Bulk, Consumer-Oriented, and Intermediate Product Exports

Table 5. U.S. Agricultural Exports, FY1990-FY2009: Total, Bulk, Consumer-Ready, and Intermediate Product Exports ($ thousands)

Year	Total	Bulk	% of Total	Consumer-Oriented	% of Total	Intermediate	% of Total
1990	40,347,960	21,793,461	54.0	9,891,735	24.5	8,662,764	21.5
1991	37,864,207	17,701,487	46.7	11,574,646	30.6	8,588,074	22.7
1992	42,554,780	19,523,240	45.9	13,689,029	32.2	9,342,511	22.0
1993	43,057,753	19,084,550	44.3	14,889,726	34.6	9,083,477	21.1
1994	43,893,020	17,940,578	40.9	16,460,463	37.5	9,491,979	21.6
1995	54,613,152	24,446,611	44.8	18,847,340	34.5	11,319,201	20.7
1996	59,785,653	28,781,235	48.1	20,167,462	33.7	10,836,956	18.1
1997	57,305,347	24,250,805	42.3	20,878,010	36.4	12,176,532	21.2
1998	53,661,663	20,925,957	39.0	20,641,538	38.5	12,094,168	22.5
1999	49,118,260	18,596,897	37.9	19,898,512	40.5	10,622,851	21.6
2000	50,761,767	18,580,955	36.6	21,481,221	42.3	10,699,591	21.1

Table 5. (Continued)

Year	Total	Bulk	% of Total	Consumer-Oriented	% of Total	Intermediate	% of Total
2001	52,716,911	18,436,458	35.0	22,541,751	42.8	11,738,702	22.3
2002	53,319,318	19,122,275	35.9	21,708,519	40.7	12,488,524	23.4
2003	56,013,986	21,224,523	37.9	22,723,487	40.6	12,065,977	21.5
2004	62,408,831	26,903,911	43.1	23,361,967	37.4	12,142,954	19.5
2005	62,516,299	23,613,456	37.8	26,287,920	42.0	12,614,923	20.2
2006	68,592,956	25,619,902	37.4	29,363,783	42.8	13,609,271	19.8
2007	82,216,762	32,883,623	40.0	33,191,509	40.4	16,141,630	19.6
2008	115,305,439	52,375,640	45.4	41,781,771	36.2	21,148,029	18.3
2009	96,632,193	38,629,929	39.9	39,538,561	40.9	18,436,703	19.1

Source: Data in this table are compiled from U.S. Department of Agriculture, Foreign Agricultural Service databases, available at *http://www.fas.usda.gov/gats/default.aspx*.

MAJOR COUNTRY MARKETS FOR U.S. AGRICULTURAL EXPORTS

- *Canada and Mexico*, both U.S. partners in the North American Free Trade Agreement (NAFTA), are the first- and second-largest markets for U.S. agricultural exports. Total U.S. agricultural exports to these two countries in FY2010 are forecast at $30.2 billion.
- *China* is the third-largest U.S. export market, with $11.7 billion expected in FY2010.
- *Japan* ($11.2 billion forecast for FY2010), which was the number one U.S. destination for agricultural products for many years, is forecast to be the fourth- largest export destination. It is followed by the EU-27, the fifth-largest U.S. farm export market, with forecast agricultural exports of $7.8 billion.
- Other Asian markets—*South Korea and Taiwan*—also are major markets for U.S. agricultural exports with forecast values in FY2010 of $4.1 billion and $3.0 billion, respectively.

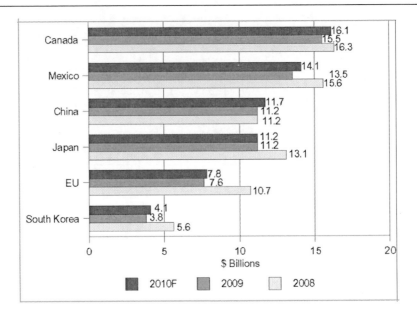

Source: U.S. Department of Agriculture. Economic Research Service. F = Forecast

Figure 6. Major Country Markets for U.S. Exports, FY2008-FY2010F.

Table 6. Major Country Markets for U.S. Agricultural Exports, FY2008-FY2010F ($ billion)

Country	2008	2009	2010F
Canada	16.3	15.5	16.1
Mexico	15.6	13.5	14.1
China	11.2	11.2	11.7
Japan	13.1	11.2	11.2
EU-27	10.7	7.6	7.8
South Korea	5.6	3.8	4.1
Taiwan	3.5	2.9	3.0
Hong Kong	1.6	1.8	1.9
Russia	1.9	1.4	1.5
Turkey	1.7	1.4	1.4

Source: U.S. Department of Agriculture. Economic Research Service, Outlook for U.S. Agricultural Trade, AES65, February 18, 2010, available at http://usda.mannlib.cornell.edu/usda/current/AES/AES-02-18-2010.pdf.

Note: F = Forecast.

WORLD EXPORT MARKET SHARES: CROPS

- **Wheat:** Although it has lost export market share over the last decade, the United States remains the major supplier of wheat and wheat products to the world market, with a forecast share of 21% in marketing year 2009/2010. The EU (16%), Canada (15%), and the Russian Federation (13%) are major competitors in this market (see **Figure 7** and **Table 7**).
- **Rice:** Thailand (34% forecast for 2009/2010) is the world's major rice exporter; but Vietnam (19%) has emerged as a major competitor. Pakistan's export market share in 2009/20 10 is forecast to be 11%. The United States is the world's fourth- largest rice exporter with a forecast share in 2009/2010 of 10% (see **Figure 8** and **Table 8**).
- **Corn:** The United States dominates the world export market for corn with a 2009/20 10 forecast export share of 64% (see **Figure 9** and **Table 9**).
- **Soybeans:** The United States is forecast to be the world's main supplier of soybeans to the world market in 2009/2010 with a share of 46%, down from 73% in 1995/1996. Over the same period, Brazil's share grew from 10.9% to 30%. (see **Figure 10** and **Table 10**).
- **Cotton:** U.S. cotton exports are estimated to be 33% of the world total in 2009/2010. U.S. competitors include India (19%), Uzbekistan (12%), and West/Central African countries (7%) (see **Figure 11** and **Table 11**).

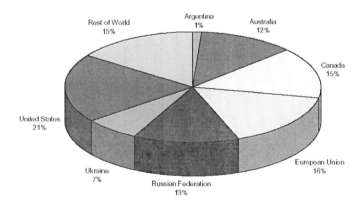

Source: U.S. Department of Agriculture, Foreign Agricultural Service. Notes: F = Forecast.

Figure 7. Shares of World Exports of Wheat and Wheat Products, 2009/2010F

Table 7. Shares of World Exports of Wheat and Wheat Products, 1995/1996-2009/2010F (percent)

Country	1995/1996	1996/1997	1997/1998	1998/1999	1999/2000	2000/2001	2001/2002
Argentina	4.5	9.7	9.4	9.0	9.9	11.1	10.8
Australia	12.2	17.5	14.7	15.8	15.3	16.3	15.3
Canada	17.2	17.4	20.4	14.1	17.3	17.0	15.5
European Union[a]	13.3	17.1	13.6	14.3	18.2	15.3	11.8
Russian Federation	0.2	0.7	1.1	1.6	0.5	0.7	4.0
Ukraine	1.4	1.2	1.3	4.6	1.7	0.1	5.1
United States	34.1	26.2	27.1	28.4	26.3	27.4	24.3
Rest of World	17.2	10.1	12.4	12.1	10.8	12.1	13.2
Country	**2002/2003**	**2003/2004**	**2004/2005**	**2005/2006**	**2006/2007**	**2007/2008**	**2008/2009E**
Argentina	5.9	7.1	11.8	7.2	10.5	8.8	6.0
Australia	10.2	14.6	13.9	13.4	9.7	6.4	9.4
Canada	8.8	15.0	13.3	13.7	16.7	14.2	13.0
European Union[a]	16.9	9.5	13.0	13.8	12.0	10.5	17.8
Russian Federation	11.8	3.0	7.4	9.2	9.2	10.8	12.9
Ukraine	6.1	0.1	3.9	5.7	2.9	1.1	9.1
United States	21.3	31.1	25.1	23.9	21.7	29.5	19.1
Rest of World	19.0	19.7	11.7	13.0	17.4	18.7	12.5
Country	**2009/2010F**						
Argentina	1.2						
Australia	11.8						
Canada	15.0						
European Union[a]	16.2						
Russian Federation	13.4						
Ukraine	6.9						
United States	20.3						
Rest of World	15.3						

Source: U.S. Department of Agriculture, Foreign Agricultural Service Production, Supply and Distribution Online database, http://www.fas.usda.gov/psdonline/psdHome.aspx.

Notes: July-June marketing year.

E = Estimate.

F = Forecast.

a. 1995/1996-1 998/1999 data are EU-15 and 1990/2000 to present are EU-27.

Table 8. Shares of World Exports of Rice, 1994/1995-2009/2010F (percent)

Country	1994/1995	1995/1996	1996/1997	1997/1998	1998/1999	1999/2000	2000/2001
China	0.2	1.3	5.0	13.5	10.9	13.0	7.6
India	20.0	18.6	11.1	16.9	11.1	6.4	7.9
Pakistan	8.5	8.5	9.4	7.2	7.4	8.9	9.9
Thailand	28.6	26.8	27.7	23.0	26.9	28.8	30.8
United States	14.6	13.3	12.2	11.5	10.7	12.5	10.4
Vietnam	11.1	15.4	17.6	13.7	18.4	14.8	14.4
Rest of World	17.1	16.1	17.0	14.2	14.7	15.7	19.1

Country	2001/2002	2002/2003	2003/2004	2004/2005	2005/2006	2006/2007	2007/2008
China	7.0	9.4	3.2	2.3	4.2	4.2	3.3
India	23.9	16.0	11.6	16.2	15.6	19.8	11.4
Pakistan	5.8	7.1	7.3	10.5	12.3	8.5	10.1
Thailand	26.0	27.4	37.2	25.1	25.3	30.0	33.8
United States	11.8	13.9	11.3	13.4	11.4	9.5	11.1
Vietnam	11.6	13.8	15.8	17.9	16.2	14.2	15.7
Rest of World	13.9	12.5	13.5	14.7	15.1	13.8	14.6

Country	2008/2009E	2009/2010F
China	2.8	4.4
India	7.1	5.1
Pakistan	10.6	11.1
Thailand	30.1	33.7
United States	11.0	10.3
Vietnam	20.2	18.5
Rest of World	18.1	16.9

Source: U.S. Department of Agriculture, Foreign Agricultural Service Production, Supply and Distribution Online database, *http://www.fas.usda.gov/psdonline/ psdHome.aspx.*
Notes: July-June marketing year.
E = Estimate.
F = Forecast.

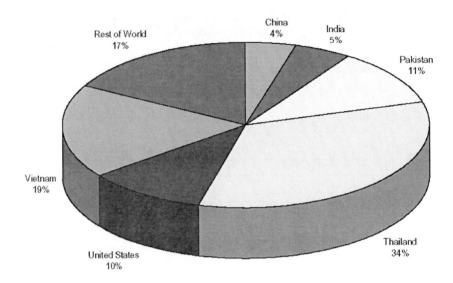

Source: U.S. Department of Agriculture, Foreign Agricultural Service.
Note: F = Forecast.

Figure 8. Shares of World Exports of Rice, 2009/2010F

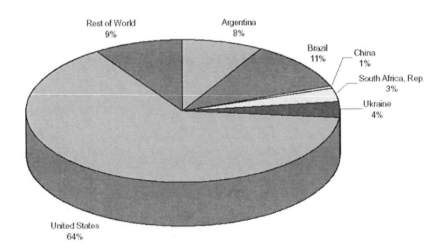

Source: U.S. Department of Agriculture, Foreign Agricultural Service.
Note: F = Forecast.

Figure 9. Shares of World Exports of Corn, 2009/2010F

Table 9. Shares of World Exports of Corn, 1995/1996-2009/2010F (percent)

Country	1995/1996	1996/1997	1997/1998	1998/1999	1999/2000	2000/2001	2001/2002
Argentina	10.7	15.3	20.2	11.4	12.3	16.1	11.8
Brazil	0.3	0.7	0.0	0.0	0.1	4.9	5.3
China	0.2	5.8	9.8	4.9	13.7	9.6	11.8
South Africa, Rep.	2.7	2.4	1.7	1.2	1.2	1.9	1.6
Ukraine	0.1	0.0	0.9	0.5	0.1	0.5	0.5
United States	81.4	70.0	59.9	75.7	68.4	63.7	64.9
Rest of World	4.5	5.7	7.5	6.3	4.3	3.3	4.1
Country	2002/2003	2003/2004	2004/2005	2005/2006	2006/2007	2007/2008	2008/2009E
Argentina	16.1	13.2	18.1	13.0	17.2	16.0	10.5
Brazil	4.1	7.4	1.9	3.4	8.8	8.0	8.9
China	19.8	9.6	10.0	4.5	5.8	0.6	0.3
South Africa, Rep.	1.5	1.0	2.0	1.7	0.5	1.1	3.1
Ukraine	1.1	1.6	3.1	3.0	1.1	2.1	6.8
United States	53.2	61.7	59.7	67.9	59.3	61.8	58.9
Rest of World	4.2	5.6	5.3	6.5	7.3	10.4	11.4
Country	2009/2010F						
Argentina	8.3						
Brazil	11.2						
China	0.6						
South Africa, Rep.	2.9						
Ukraine	3.5						
United States	64.3						
Rest of World	9.2						

Source: U.S. Department of Agriculture, Foreign Agricultural Service Production, Supply and Distribution Online database, *http://www.fas.usda.gov/psdonline/ psdHome.aspx*.

Notes: October-September marketing year.

E = Estimate.

F = Forecast.

Table 10. Shares of World Exports of Soybeans, 1995/1996-2009/2010F (percent)

Country	1995/ 1996	1996/ 1997	1997/ 1998	1998/ 1999	1999/ 2000	2000/ 2001	2001/ 2002
Argentina	6.6	2.1	7.2	8.1	9.0	13.6	11.3
Brazil	10.9	22.9	22.3	23.5	24.3	28.8	27.4
Canada	1.9	1.3	2.0	2.3	2.1	1.4	0.9
Paraguay	5.0	5.8	5.8	6.1	4.4	4.7	4.3
United States	73.0	65.6	60.5	57.7	58.2	50.4	54.7
Rest of World	2.5	2.3	2.2	2.3	1.9	1.2	1.3
Country	2002/ 2003	2003/ 2004	2004/ 2005	2005/ 2006	2006/ 2007	2007/ 2008	2008/ 2009E
Argentina	14.1	12.0	14.8	11.4	13.4	17.4	7.7
Brazil	32.2	36.4	31.1	40.6	32.9	31.9	39.0
Canada	1.2	1.6	1.7	2.1	2.4	2.2	2.6
Paraguay	4.6	4.7	4.5	3.7	6.1	6.8	3.1
United States	46.6	43.1	46.1	40.1	42.6	39.7	45.3
Rest of World	1.3	2.1	1.8	2.1	2.6	2.0	2.4
Country	2009/ 2010F						
Argentina	12.5						
Brazil	30.4						
Canada	2.6						
Paraguay	6.3						
United States	45.6						
Rest of World	2.7						

Source: U.S. Department of Agriculture, Foreign Agricultural Service Production, Supply and Distribution Online database, http://www.fas.usda.gov/psdonline/ psdHome.aspx.
Notes: Marketing year.
E = Estimate
F = Forecast

Table 11. Shares of World Exports of Cotton, 1995/1996-2009/2010F (percent)

Country	1995/ 1996	1996/ 1997	1997/ 1998	1998/ 1999	1999/ 2000	2000/ 2001	2001/ 2002
Australia	5.3	8.9	10.1	12.9	11.8	14.9	10.7
West/Central Africa[a]	10.2	12.3	13.5	15.3	13.8	12.4	12.2
India	2.1	4.4	1.2	0.8	0.3	0.4	0.2
United States	28.1	25.6	28.1	18.3	24.8	25.7	37.7
Uzbekistan	16.5	17.0	17.1	16.2	15.5	13.2	12.0

Table 11. (Continued)

Country	1995/ 1996	1996/ 1997	1997/ 1998	1998/ 1999	1999/ 2000	2000/ 2001	2001/ 2002
Rest of World	37.8	31.8	30.0	36.5	33.9	33.4	27.1

Country	2002/ 2003	2003/ 2004	2004/ 2005	2005/ 2006	2006/ 007	2007/ 2008	2008/ 2009E
Australia	8.7	6.5	5.7	6.5	5.7	3.2	4.1
West/Central Africa[a]	12.4	13.4	11.8	10.0	10.3	6.7	7.3
India	0.2	2.1	1.9	7.7	12.3	18.3	7.8
United States	39.1	41.4	41.2	39.4	35.1	35.6	44.8
Uzbekistan	11.2	9.3	11.3	10.8	12.2	11.0	8.8
Rest of World	28.4	27.3	28.1	25.7	24.4	25.2	27.2

Country	2009/2010F						
Australia	5.0						
West/Central Africa[a]	6.9						
India	19.4						
United States	32.9						
Uzbekistan	12.2						
Rest of World	23.6						

Source: U.S. Department of Agriculture, Foreign Agricultural Service Production, Supply and Distribution Online database, http://www.fas.usda.gov/psdonline/ psdHome.aspx.

Notes: Marketing year.

E = Estimate.

F = Forecast.

a. Includes Benin, Burkina Faso, Cameroon, Central African Republic, Chad, Cote d'Ivoire, Mali, Niger, Senegal, and Togo.

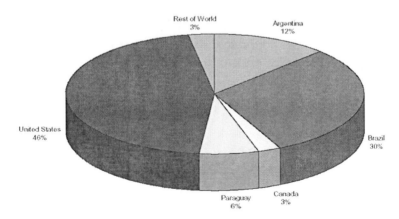

Source: U.S. Department of Agriculture, Foreign Agricultural Service.
Note: F = Forecast.

Figure 10. Shares of World Exports of Soybeans, 2009/2010F

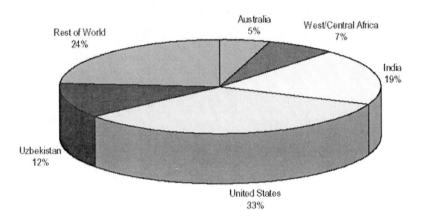

Source: U.S. Department of Agriculture, Foreign Agricultural Service.
Notes: West/Central Africa includes Benin, Burkina Faso, Cameroon, Central African Republic, Chad, Cote d'Ivoire, Mali, Niger, Senegal, and Togo.
F = Forecast.

Figure 11. Shares of World Exports of Cotton, 2009/2010F

WORLD MARKET SHARES: LIVESTOCK AND DAIRY

- **Beef:** Brazil, with 26% (forecast) of world exports in 2010, has emerged as the world's largest supplier of beef to world markets. The U.S. share of world beef exports is forecast to be 12% in 2010. Lingering effects of mad cow disease continue to affect demand for U.S. beef in world markets; the U.S. share of world beef exports had reached 19% in 2000. (See **Figure 12** and **Table 12**).
- **Pork:** Taiwan (36%) and the EU (21%) are forecast to be the world's largest exporters of pork in 2010 (**Figure 13** and **Table 13**).
- **Poultry:** Brazil is the world's leading supplier of poultry meat on the world market (40% forecast for 2010). The United States, with 34% of world poultry meat exports, and the EU (9%) have lost market share to Brazil in recent years (**Figure 14** and **Table 14**).
- **Dairy Products:** For 2009, New Zealand (29%) and the United States (18%) are forecast to be the leading suppliers of nonfat dry milk to world markets. The EU (40%) dominates the world market for cheese, while New Zealand (5 8%) is the world's largest exporter of butter.

Table 12. Shares of World Exports of Beef and Veal, 1995-2010F (percent)

Country	1995	1996	1997	1998	1999	2000	2001
Argentina	9.8	9.5	7.8	5.5	6.0	6.0	2.9
European Union[a]	22.0	21.1	18.8	14.2	17.3	11.2	10.4
United States	15.1	16.3	16.7	18.0	18.6	18.9	17.6
Brazil	4.2	4.3	4.0	5.5	7.8	8.2	12.7
Australia	20.3	19.7	20.1	22.7	21.3	22.2	23.5
New Zealand	9.1	9.6	8.6	8.7	7.4	8.0	8.3
Rest of World	19.5	19.5	24.0	25.3	21.5	25.5	24.7
Country	**2002**	**2003**	**2004**	**2005**	**2006**	**2007**	**2008**
Argentina	5.4	5.9	9.3	10.3	7.4	7.1	5.6
European Union[a]	9.0	6.7	5.5	3.5	2.9	1.8	2.7
United States	17.3	17.6	3.1	4.3	6.9	8.6	11.4
Brazil	13.6	17.9	24.2	25.2	27.8	28.9	24.0
Australia	20.9	19.1	20.6	19.0	19.1	18.5	18.8
New Zealand	7.4	8.4	8.9	7.9	7.1	6.6	7.1
Rest of World	26.6	24.4	28.5	29.8	28.9	28.6	30.3
Country	**2009P**	**2010F**					
Argentina	7.9	5.4					
European Union[a]	2.3	2.2					
United States	11.0	11.6					
Brazil	21.9	26.0					
Australia	19.5	18.7					
New Zealand	7.4	7.2					
Rest of World	30.0	28.9					

Source: U.S. Department of Agriculture, Foreign Agricultural Service Production, Supply and Distribution Online database, *http://www.fas.usda.gov/psdonline/ psdHome.aspx*.
Notes:
P = Preliminary.
F = Forecast.
a. 1995-1998 data are EU-15 and 1999 to present are EU-27.

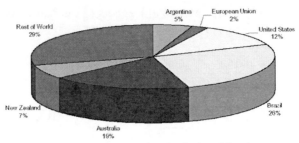

Source: U.S. Department of Agriculture, Foreign Agricultural Service.
Note: F = Forecast.

Figure 12. Shares of World Exports of Beef and Veal, 2010F

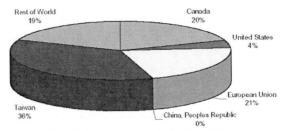

Source: U.S. Department of Agriculture, Foreign Agricultural Service.
Note: F = Forecast.

Figure 13. Shares of World Pork Exports, 2010F

Table 13. Shares of World Pork Exports, 1994-2010F (percent)

Country	1995	1996	1997	1998	1999	2000	2001
Canada	15.5	13.6	14.4	14.7	17.0	21.4	22.7
United States	4.4	4.8	6.9	6.9	4.4	4.7	7.0
European Union[a]	32.6	30.5	32.6	35.1	49.0	43.3	30.2
China	16.1	13.7	2.2	0.1	0.0	0.0	0.1
Taiwan	15.1	15.6	16.2	19.0	17.9	18.9	21.8
Rest of World	16.3	21.8	27.6	24.3	29.6	30.6	40.0
Country	**2002**	**2003**	**2004**	**2005**	**2006**	**2007**	**2008**
Canada	23.1	23.3	20.6	21.7	20.7	20.0	18.4
United States	8.2	9.5	11.4	10.0	10.4	6.8	3.6
European Union[a]	26.6	27.3	27.6	22.8	24.6	24.9	28.1
China	0.1	0.0	0.0	0.0	0.0	0.0	0.0
Taiwan	19.6	18.7	21.0	24.2	26.0	27.6	34.4
Rest of World	42.0	21.1	19.4	21.3	18.3	20.7	15.4

Table 13. (Continued)

Country	2009P	2010F				
Canada	20.7	19.6				
United States	4.2	4.3				
European Union[a]	22.9	21.4				
China	0.0	0.0				
Taiwan	34.5	36.0				
Rest of World	17.7	18.7				

Source: U.S. Department of Agriculture, Foreign Agricultural Service Production, Supply and Distribution Online database, *http://www.fas.usda.gov/psdonline/ psdHome.aspx*.
Notes: F = Forecast.
a. 1995-1998 data are EU-15 and 1999 to present are EU-27.

Table 14. Shares of World Total Poultry Meat Exports, 1994-2010F (percent)

Country	1995	1996	1997	1998	1999	2000	2001
United States	41.3	41.9	48.8	46.8	47.3	46.8	46.0
Brazil	10.0	11.7	15.1	13.8	16.7	18.3	22.4
European Union[a]	NA	NA	17.8	19.0	17.7	15.2	11.8
China	6.2	6.6	8.1	7.6	8.5	9.7	8.9
Rest of World	42.5	39.8	10.2	12.8	9.7	10.0	10.9
Country	**2002**	**2003**	**2004**	**2005**	**2006**	**2007**	**2008**
United States	38.7	37.1	35.8	34.5	36.0	36.3	37.5
Brazil	28.0	31.7	39.9	40.1	38.2	39.6	38.5
European Union[a]	13.6	12.0	12.0	10.2	10.5	8.6	8.8
China	7.8	6.5	4.0	4.9	4.9	4.8	3.4
Rest of World	12.0	12.7	8.3	10.3	10.4	10.7	11.8
Country	**2009F**	**2010P**					
United States	36.6	34.3					
Brazil	38.5	40.1					
European Union[a]	8.8	8.6					
China	3.1	3.0					
Rest of World	13.0	13.9					

Source: U.S. Department of Agriculture, Foreign Agricultural Service Production, Supply and Distribution Online database, *http://www.fas.usda.gov/psdonline/ psdHome.aspx*.
Notes: NA = Not Available.
P = Preliminary.
F = Forecast.
a. 1997-1998 data are EU-15 and 1999 to present are EU-27.

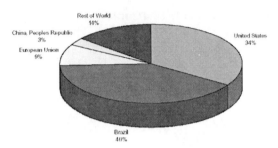

Source: U.S. Department of Agriculture, Foreign Agricultural Service.
Note: F = Forecast.

Figure 14. Shares of World Poultry Meat Exports, 2010F

Table 15. Shares of World Nonfat Dry Milk Exports, 1995-2009F (percent)

Country	1995	1996	1997	1998	1999	2000	2001
Canada	2.5	2.5	2.9	3.8	2.7	1.9	3.7
United States	9.5	2.4	11.3	11.5	14.4	8.5	7.7
European Union[a]	NA	NA	27.3	19.4	24.4	27.1	22.3
Australia	10.9	12.8	19.8	22.1	15.9	15.2	17.5
New Zealand	9.7	11.5	20.7	21.8	13.6	10.5	15.6
Rest of World	67.4	70.8	18.0	21.4	29.1	36.7	33.3
Country	**2002**	**2003**	**2004**	**2005**	**2006**	**2007**	**2008**
Canada	3.7	2.4	1.1	0.5	1.2	1.1	1.4
United States	9.6	9.3	15.9	23.0	26.1	20.6	35.4
European Union[a]	19.9	22.2	19.1	15.8	8.0	16.3	16.2
Australia	17.6	12.7	12.9	11.7	17.2	14.1	10.8
New Zealand	18.9	20.7	21.0	18.4	22.1	26.4	22.7
Rest of World	30.3	32.8	30.0	30.5	25.5	21.3	13.6
Country	**2009F**						
Canada	1.2						
United States	18.2						
European Union[a]	16.4						
Australia	15.5						
New Zealand	28.2						
Rest of World	20.6						

Source: U.S. Department of Agriculture, Foreign Agricultural Service Production, Supply and Distribution Online database, http://www.fas.usda.gov/psdonline/psdHome.aspx.
Notes: NA = Not Available. P = Preliminary. F = Forecast.
a. 1997-1998 data are EU-15 and 1999 to present are EU-27.

Table 16. Shares of World Cheese Exports, 1994-2009F (percent)

Country	1994	1995	1996	1997	1998	1999	2000	2001
European Union[a]	NA	NA	NA	51.0	46.2	45.2	31.1	30.8
New Zealand[b]	5.9	6.9	6.7	25.0	25.6	26.1	16.3	16.0
Australia[c]	4.1	4.5	4.3	13.3	16.6	18.7	14.4	13.9
Ukraine	0.2	0.2	0.1	0.2	0.4	0.7	0.8	2.0
United States	1.1	1.1	1.2	4.0	4.1	4.1	3.0	3.4
Argentina	0.6	0.5	0.4	2.0	1.9	2.2	1.4	1.1
Canada	0.3	0.6	0.6	2.4	3.0	2.7	1.2	1.2
Country	**1994**	**1995**	**1996**	**1997**	**1998**	**1999**	**2000**	**2001**
Rest of World	87.8	86.2	86.6	2.0	2.2	0.3	31.8	31.5
Country	**2002**	**2003**	**2004**	**2005**	**2006**	**2007**	**2008**	**2009F**
European Union[a]	30.3	31.3	29.7	28.7	31.7	28.8	39.2	40.6
New Zealand[b]	16.7	16.9	16.4	15.2	15.1	16.7	22.6	22.8
Australia[c]	13.1	12.0	12.0	13.1	11.4	11.4	16.2	15.0
Ukraine	2.2	3.5	5.3	6.7	2.8	3.3	6.2	5.9
United States	3.3	3.0	3.5	3.3	4.0	5.3	10.5	8.5
Argentina	1.6	1.3	1.8	2.6	3.3	2.4	2.9	4.7
Canada	1.0	0.6	0.6	0.5	0.5	0.5	0.8	0.7
Rest of World	31.8	31.2	30.8	29.9	31.2	31.4	1.6	1.9

Source: U.S. Department of Agriculture, Foreign Agricultural Service Production, Supply and Distribution Online database, http://www.fas.usda.gov/psdonline/ psdHome.aspx.
Notes: NA = Not Available. P = Preliminary. F = Forecast.
a. 1997-1998 data are EU-15 and 1999 to present are EU-27.
b. Year ending May 31 of the year shown.
c. Year ending June 30 of the year shown.

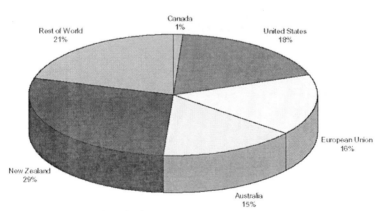

Source: U.S. Department of Agriculture, Foreign Agricultural Service.
Note: F = Forecast.

Figure 15. Shares of World Nonfat Dry Milk Exports, 2009F

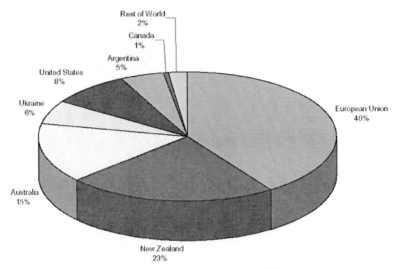

Source: U.S. Department of Agriculture, Foreign Agricultural Service.
Note: F = Forecast.

Figure 16. Shares of World Cheese Exports, 2009F

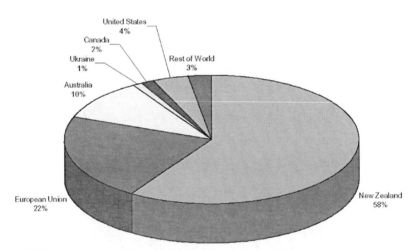

Source: U.S. Department of Agriculture, Foreign Agricultural Service.
Note: F = Forecast.

Figure 17. Shares of World Butter Exports, 2009F

Table 17. Shares of World Butter Exports, 1994-2009F (percent)

Country	1994	1995	1996	1997	1998	1999	2000	2001
New Zealand[a]	20.2	19.3	21.0	42.1	50.2	34.1	37.0	36.4
European Union[b]	NA	NA	NA	29.2	26.8	24.5	21.4	21.7
Australia[c]	7.1	6.9	6.6	14.8	16.7	14.3	15.2	12.9
Ukraine	1.7	5.6	8.4	7.9	1.6	1.0	3.4	5.6
Canada	0.2	0.5	1.1	1.6	1.9	1.3	1.1	1.7
United States	7.1	5.2	1.7	2.4	0.5	0.2	0.4	0.0
Rest of World	63.7	62.5	61.1	2.0	2.2	24.5	21.5	21.6
Country	**2002**	**2003**	**2004**	**2005**	**2006**	**2007**	**2008**	**2009F**
New Zealand[a]	36.1	33.6	31.8	27.8	36.3	41.0	51.8	59.0
European Union[b]	23.5	27.0	28.1	29.9	24.6	20.2	21.3	21.9
Australia[c]	12.8	9.3	6.0	6.2	8.1	7.5	8.3	10.2
Ukraine	1.5	1.5	3.3	2.1	1.8	0.4	1.0	1.0
Canada	1.7	1.0	1.4	1.8	1.8	1.2	0.4	1.6
United States	0.3	1.0	0.7	0.8	1.1	3.8	14.8	3.6
Rest of World	24.0	26.6	28.8	31.5	26.3	26.0	2.4	2.6

Source: U.S. Department of Agriculture, Foreign Agricultural Service Production, Supply and Distribution Online database, http://www.fas.usda.gov/psdonline/ psdHome.aspx.
Notes: NA = Not Available.
P = Preliminary.
F = Forecast.
a. Year ending May 31 of the year shown.
b. 1997-1998 data are EU- 15 and 1999 to present are EU-27.
c. Year ending June 30 of the year shown.

WORLD MARKET SHARES: SUGAR

- Brazil is the world's leading exporter of sugar with an export market share forecast at 48% for 2009/2010.
- Australia, with 7% of global sugar exports, is the world's second-largest exporter of sugar.
- Sugar exports from the United States, a sugar importer, are negligible (only 0.4% forecast for 2009/2010).

Table 18. Shares of World Centrifugal Sugar Exports, 1995/1996-2009/2010F (percent)

Country	1995/1996	1996/1997	1997/1998	1998/1999	1999/2000	2000/2001	2001/2002
United States	0.9	0.5	0.4	0.6	0.3	0.3	0.3
Mexico	1.8	2.5	2.9	1.4	0.8	0.4	1.0
Total Caribbean	12.7	11.3	8.0	9.7	9.5	9.0	8.4
DR-CAFTA[a]	5.2	5.7	6.3	5.2	5.2	6.1	5.3
Brazil	16.4	15.3	19.1	23.2	27.1	20.1	27.4
European Union[b]	13.1	13.8	16.9	14.2	14.7	17.3	11.3
Australia	12.0	12.0	12.1	10.8	9.9	8.0	8.5
Rest of World	37.8	38.9	34.4	35.0	32.6	38.8	37.8

Country	2002/2003	2003/2004	2004/2005	2005/2006	2006/2007	2007/2008	2008/2009P
United States	0.3	0.6	0.5	0.4	0.8	0.4	0.2
Mexico	0.1	0.0	0.3	1.7	0.3	1.3	1.8
Total Caribbean	4.8	5.2	2.5	2.6	2.2	2.6	2.8
DR-CAFTA[a]	5.0	5.2	5.5	5.4	5.3	4.6	5.3
Brazil	29.4	32.7	38.4	34.2	41.2	37.9	42.0
European Union[b]	11.8	10.5	12.8	16.7	4.3	2.7	3.5
Australia	8.7	8.9	9.5	8.4	7.6	7.1	7.3
Rest of World	40.0	36.9	30.5	30.7	38.4	43.4	37.1

Country	2009/2010F
United States	0.4
Mexico	0.3
Total Caribbean	2.6
DR-CAFTA[a]	5.1
Brazil	47.4
European Union[b]	2.9
Australia	7.0
Rest of World	34.4

Source: U.S. Department of Agriculture. Foreign Agricultural Service Production, Supply and Distribution Online database, http://www.fas.usda.gov/psdonline/psdHome.aspx.

Notes: P = Preliminary. F = Forecast.

a. DR-CAFTA includes Dominican Republic and Central America. 1995/1996-2003/2004 data are EU-15, 2004/2005-2005/2006 are EU-25, and 2006/2007 to present are EU-27.

b. The EU Includes French overseas departments of Reunion, Guadeloupe, and Martinique. EU trade data does not Include intra trade. Beginning 2004/2005, the data reflects the EU enlargement by accession of 10 countries. EU exports include sugar-containing products.

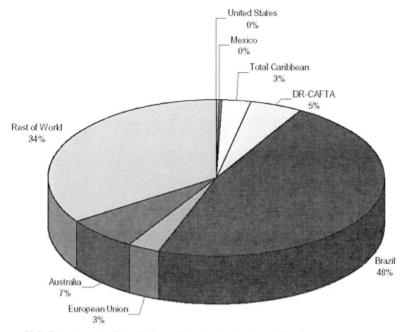

Source: U.S. Department of Agriculture, Foreign Agricultural Service.
Notes: DR-CAFTA includes Dominican Republic and Central America. The European Union (EU) data include French overseas departments of Reunion, Guadeloupe, and Martinique, but do not include intra trade. EU data include sugar-containing products. October-September marketing year. F = Forecast.

Figure 18. Shares of World Centrifugal Sugar Exports, 2009/2010F

MAJOR U.S. AGRICULTURAL IMPORTS

- High-value horticultural products (fruits, vegetables, nuts, wine, beer, nursery stock and flowers, and others) are the largest category of U.S. agricultural imports, with more than $34 billion forecast for FY2010.
- Other sizeable commodity imports forecast for FY20010 are grains and feeds ($7.6 billion), livestock, dairy, and poultry ($11.3 billion), and oilseeds and products ($6.0 billion).
- Imports of tropical products such as coffee, cocoa, sugar, and rubber are forecast to be $16.5 billion in FY2010.

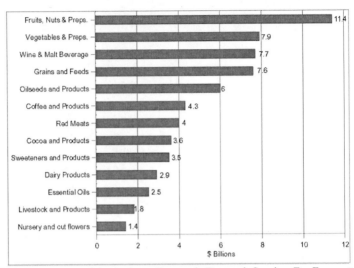

Source: U.S. Department of Agriculture. Economic Research Service. F = Forecast

Figure 19. Major Agricultural Imports by Commodity, FY2010F

Table 19. Major U.S. Agricultural Imports, FY2010F ($ billions)

Commodity	FY2010F Imports
Fruits, Nuts & Preps.	11.4
Vegetables & Preps.	7.9
Wine & Malt Beverage	7.7
Grains and Feeds	7.6
Oilseeds and Products	6.0
Coffee and Products	4.3
Red Meats	4.0
Cocoa and Products	3.6
Sweeteners and Products	3.5
Dairy Products	2.9
Essential Oils	2.5
Livestock and Products	1.8
Nursery and Cut Flowers	1.4

Source: U.S. Department of Agriculture, Economic Research Service, Outlook for U.S. Agricultural Trade, AES65, February 18, 2010, available at *http://usda.mannlib.cornell.edu/usda/current/AES/AES-02-18-2010.pdf.*

Note: F = Forecast.

U.S. AGRICULTURAL IMPORTS BY COUNTRY OF ORIGIN

- NAFTA partners Canada ($16 billion) and Mexico ($12 billion) and the EU-27 ($14 billion) are forecast to be the source of 70 % of total U.S. agricultural imports in FY2010.
- Agricultural imports from Brazil also are expected to reach a forecast $2.6 billion in FY2010, making it the fourth-largest source of U.S. agricultural imports.
- Australia (at $2.5 billion), with whom the United States entered a free trade agreement (FTA) in 2005, is forecast to be the fifth-largest supplier in FY2009.

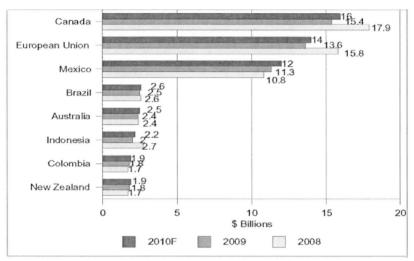

Source: U.S. Department of Agriculture. Economic Research Service. F = Forecast

Figure 20. U.S. Agricultural Imports by Country of Origin, FY2008-FY2010F

Table 20. U.S. Agricultural Imports by Country of Origin, FY2008-FY2010F ($ billion)

Country	FY2008	FY2009	FY2010F
European Union	15.8	13.6	14.0
Canada	17.9	15.4	16.0
Mexico	10.8	11.3	12.0
Brazil	2.6	2.5	2.6

Table 20. (Continued)

Country	FY2008	FY2009	FY2010F
Australia	2.4	2.4	2.5
Indonesia	2.7	2.0	2.2
New Zealand	1.7	1.8	1.9
Colombia	1.7	1.8	1.9

Source: U.S. Department of Agriculture, Economic Research Service, Outlook for U.S. Agricultural Trade, AES65, February 18, 2010, available at http://usda.mannlib.cornell.edu/usda/current/AES/AES-02-18-2010.pdf.
Notes: F = Forecast.

REGIONAL MARKET GROWTH IN U.S. AGRICULTURAL EXPORTS

- Economic growth in Asia has contributed to relatively consistent long-term growth in U.S. agricultural exports to the region.
- Despite some year-to-year variation, the EU, the United States' fifth-largest agricultural export market, has been a relatively stable market for U.S. agricultural exports with little growth since 1992.
- Agricultural exports to countries in the former Soviet Union have declined in value since the 1992 break-up of the USSR.
- Agricultural exports to Latin America, including Mexico, and to Canada have grown rapidly since the early 1990s because of geographic proximity, NAFTA, and other factors.

Table 21. Change in U.S. Agricultural Exports to Selected Markets, FY1992-FY2010F ($ billion)

Year	Asia	European Union	Latin America[a]	Former Soviet Union	Canada
1992	17.8	7.2	6.5	2.2	4.8
1993	17.8	7.2	6.9	1.6	5.2
1994	19.9	6.6	7.4	1.0	5.3
1995	24.0	8.4	8.2	1.2	5.8
1996	26.0	9.2	9.9	1.6	6.0
1997	23.9	9.0	10.0	1.3	6.6
1998	19.7	8.5	11.3	1.0	7.0

Table 21. (Continued)

Year	Asia	European Union	Latin America[a]	Former Soviet Union	Canada
1999	18.5	7.0	10.4	0.8	7.0
2000	19.7	6.4	10.6	0.7	7.5
2001	20.1	6.5	11.6	1.1	8.0
2002	19.5	6.5	11.5	0.7	8.6
2003	21.7	6.3	12.4	0.7	9.1
2004	24.3	7.0	13.6	1.1	9.6
2005	22.5	7.2	14.4	1.2	10.4
2006	24.9	7.2	16.5	1.1	11.6
2007	29.3	8.0	20.0	1.4	13.3
2008	43.2	10.7	27.5	2.3	16.2
2009	37.8	7.6	22.8	1.8	15.5
2010F	38.0	7.7	23.6	1.7	15.7
Rate of Growth[b]	4.07%	0.35%	7.02%	-1.35%	6.44%

Source: U. S. Department of Agriculture, Economic Research Service, Outlook for U.S. Agricultural Trade, AES65, February 18, 2010, available at http://usda.mannlib.cornell.edu/usda/current/AES/AES-02-18-2010.pdf.

Notes: F = Forecast.

a. Including Mexico.

b. The rate of growth is the change in U.S. exports from 1992 to 2010F. Calculations were made by CRS using a compound rate of growth calculator.

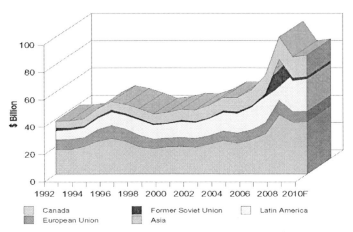

Source: U.S. Department of Agriculture. Economic Research Service. F = Forecast

Figure 21. Growth in U.S. Agricultural Exports, FY1992-FY2010F

GROWTH IN U.S. AGRICULTURAL EXPORTS TO ASIAN MARKETS

- Like the EU, Japan also has been a relatively stable and slow-growing market for U.S. agricultural exports.
- U.S. agricultural exports to China, fueled by rates of GDP growth in excess of 9%, have grown rapidly since the early 1990s (15.7%). Despite China's slower economic growth in 2009, FY2010 U.S. agricultural exports to that country are forecast to be more than five times their value in FY200 1, when China became a member of the World Trade Organization.
- Rapid income growth in Southeast Asia also has stimulated demand for U.S. agricultural exports since 1992.
- Agricultural exports to South Asia have shown slow but steady growth since 1992.

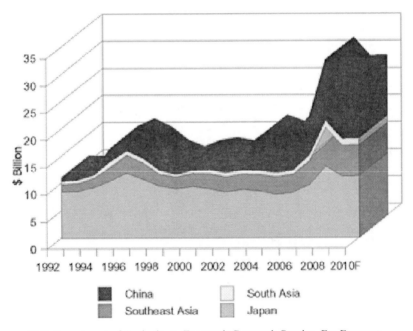

Source: U.S. Department of Agriculture. Economic Research Service. F = Forecast

Figure 22. Growth in Agricultural Exports to Asian Markets, FY1992-FY2010F

Table 22. Change in U.S. Agricultural Exports to Asian Markets, FY1992-FY2010F ($ billion)

Year	Japan	Southeast Asia	South Asia	China
1992	8.4	1.5	0.5	0.7
1993	8.5	1.6	0.6	0.3
1994	9.2	1.8	0.6	0.9
1995	10.5	2.6	1.0	2.4
1996	11.9	3.4	0.7	1.8
1997	10.7	3.1	0.7	1.8
1998	9.5	2.3	0.6	1.5
1999	8.9	2.2	0.5	1.0
2000	9.4	2.6	0.4	1.5
2001	8.9	2.9	0.6	1.9
2002	8.3	2.9	0.8	1.8
2003	8.8	2.9	0.6	3.5
2004	8.5	3.1	0.7	6.1
2005	7.8	3.4	0.7	5.3
2006	8.2	3.4	0.7	6.6
2007	9.7	4.4	1.0	7.1
2008	13.1	7.1	1.2	11.2
2009	11.2	5.7	1.2	11.2
2010F	11.3	5.7	1.2	11.2
Rate of Growth[a]	1.57%	7.28%	4.72%	15.71%

Source: U.S. Department of Agriculture. Economic Research Service, Outlook for U.S. Agricultural Trade, AES65, February 18, 2010, available at http://usda.mannlib.cornell.edu/usda/current/AES/ AES-02-18-2010.pdf.

Notes: F = Forecast.

a. The rate of growth is the change in U.S. exports from 1992 to 2010F. Calculations were made by CRS using a compound rate of growth calculator.

GROWTH IN AGRICULTURAL EXPORTS TO NORTH AND SOUTH AMERICA

- Growth in U.S. agricultural trade with Canada and Mexico, both NAFTA trading partners, and with Latin America has been particularly strong since 1992.
- U.S. agricultural exports to Canada are forecast to be $15.7 billion in FY2010.
- U.S. agricultural exports to Mexico are expected to be $14 billion in FY2010.

- U.S. agricultural exports to Latin America (excluding Mexico) are expected to reach $9.6 billion in FY2010, down from $12 billion in FY2008.

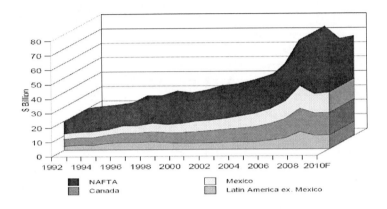

Source: U.S. Department of Agriculture. Economic Research Service. F = Forecast

Figure 23. Change in Agricultural Exports to North and South America, FY1992-FY2010F

Table 23. Change in Agricultural Exports to North and South America, FY1992-FY2010F ($ billion)

Year	Latin America ex. Mexico	Canada	Mexico	NAFTA
1992	2.8	4.8	3.7	8.5
1993	3.3	5.2	3.7	8.9
1994	3.2	5.3	4.1	9.4
1995	4.5	5.8	3.7	9.5
1996	4.9	6.6	5.1	11.7
1997	4.9	6.6	5.1	11.7
1998	5.3	7.0	6.0	13.0
1999	4.7	7.0	5.7	12.7
2000	4.3	7.5	6.3	13.8
2001	4.3	8.0	7.3	15.3
2002	4.5	8.6	7.1	15.7
2003	4.8	9.1	7.6	16.7
2004	5.2	9.6	8.4	18.0
2005	5.2	10.4	9.3	19.7

Table 23. (Continued)

Year	Latin America ex. Mexico	Canada	Mexico	NAFTA
2006	6.1	11.6	10.4	22.0
2007	7.7	13.3	12.3	25.6
2008	12.0	16.2	15.6	31.8
2009	9.3	15.5	13.5	29.0
2010F	9.6	15.7	14.0	29.7
Rate of Growth[a]	6.70%	6.44%	7.25%	6.81%

Source: U.S. Department of Agriculture, Economic Research Service, Outlook for U.S. Agricultural Trade, AES65, February 18, 2010, available at *http://usda.mannlib.cornell.edu/usda/current/AES/AES-02-18-2010.pdf*.

Notes: F = Forecast.

a. The rate of growth is the change in U.S. exports from 1992 to 2010F. Calculations were made by CRS using a compound rate of growth calculator.

U.S. AGRICULTURAL AND TRADE POLICIES

Domestic Support

The Food, Conservation, and Energy Act of 2008 (P.L. 110-246, 2008 farm bill) was enacted into law in June 2008 and will govern most federal farm and food policies through 2012. The 2008 farm bill provides support for commodities through 2012 as well as for trade and food aid programs administered by USDA.

By one widely used measure, the producer support estimate (PSE) calculated by the Organization for Economic Cooperation and Development (OECD), the United States provided $23 billion in direct payments and commodity price supports to producers in 2008 (provisional estimate).[1] PSEs measure assistance to producers in terms of the value of monetary transfers generated by agricultural policy. Transfers are paid by consumers or by taxpayers in the form of market price support, direct payments, or other support. They are a broader measure of support than direct government spending alone. The percentage PSE measures support in relation to gross farm receipts. As a percent of gross farm receipts, the PSE for the United States is 7%, the third-lowest among OECD countries (**Figure 24, Table 24**). OECD attributes the relatively low PSE expected for the United States for

2008 to a fall in commodity prices rather than to policy changes. Sugar is the most highly subsidized product in the United States, with a provisional single commodity transfer estimated at 27% of the gross value of sugar production in 2008 (**Figure 25, Table 25**).

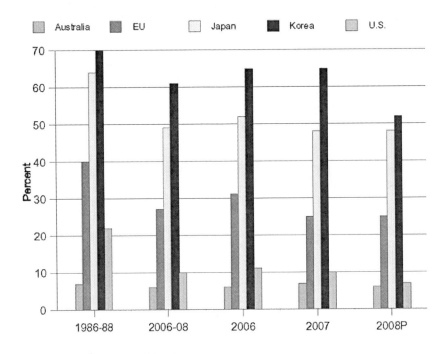

Source: OECD 2009 P = Provisional

Figure 24. Producer Support Estimates (PSEs) in Selected OECD Countries

Table 24. Producer Support Estimates (PSEs) in Selected OECD Countries (percent)

Country	1986-1988	2006-2008	2006	2007	2008P
Australia	7	6	6	7	6
EU	40	27	31	25	25
Japan	64	49	52	48	48
Korea	70	61	65	65	52
U.S.	22	10	11	10	7

Source: Organization for Economic Co-operation and Development (OECD), Agricultural Policies in OECD Countries: Monitoring and Evaluation, 2009.

Note: P = Provisional.

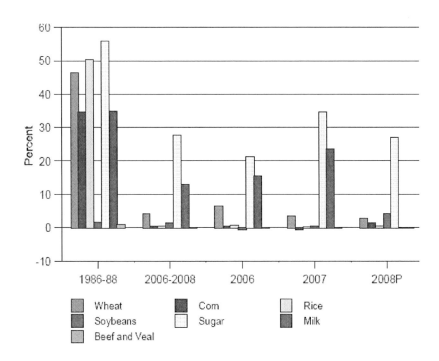

Source: OECD 2009 P = Provisional

Figure 25. Producer Single Commodity Transfers (PSCs): Selected Commodities in the United States

Table 25. Producer Single Commodity Transfers (PSC) in the United States, by Commodity (percent)

Products	1986-1988 (Average)	2006-2008	2006	2007	2008P
Wheat	46.5	4.3	6.6	3.6	2.9
Corn	34.8	0.5	0.4	-0.5	1.5
Rice	50.2	0.5	0.9	0.3	0.4
Soybeans	1.7	1.5	-0.4	0.6	4.3
Sugar	55.9	27.8	21.4	34.8	27.0
Milk	34.9	13.1	15.6	23.6	0.0
Beef and Veal	1.1	0.0	0.0	0.0	0.0

Source: Organization for Economic Cooperation and Development (OECD), Agricultural Policies in OECD Countries: Monitoring and Evaluation, 2009 edition.

Note: P = Provisional.

Trade Measures

The United States applies tariffs and tariff quotas[2] to products entering the United States from abroad. According to the World Trade Organization (WTO), the United States average applied tariff for agricultural products in 2007 was 8.9%, which is slightly above the average applied tariff for non-agricultural products (4%).[3] About 200 tariff lines (a tariff line is a product as described in a schedule or list of tariffs) are subject to tariff quotas, including beef, dairy products, and sugar. The average in-quota tariff was 9.1% in 2007, while the out-of-quota was 42%.[4]

Under the WTO Agreement on Agriculture, the United States made export subsidy reduction commitments for 13 commodities.[5] The 2008 farm bill repealed authority for the Export Enhancement Program (EEP), which was used to fund subsidies for those products, with the exception of dairy products. Export subsidies, in the form of cash bonuses, can be provided to exporters of dairy products under the Dairy Export Incentive Program (DEIP), which was reauthorized in the 2008 farm bill through 2012. Prior to its repeal, no expenditures were made for EEP from FY2002. No subsidies have been provided under DEIP since FY2004. Spurred by declining prices for dairy products in 2008-2009, USDA announced in May 2009 DEIP allocations for nonfat dry milk, butter fat, and cheeses.

A federally chartered public corporation operated by USDA, the Commodity Credit Corporation (CCC), makes credit guarantees available to private financial institutions who finance the purchase of U.S. agricultural exports. The CCC operates two export credit guarantee programs. Under GSM-102, the CCC guarantees repayment of credit made available to finance U.S. agricultural exports on credit terms of up to three years. The Facilities Guarantee Program (FGP) guarantees credit to U.S. banks that finance export sales of U.S. goods and services that are used to improve agricultural export-related facilities in emerging markets (storage, processing, and handling facilities).

Export market development programs, the Market Access Program (MAP), and the Foreign Market Development Program (FMDP) assist producer groups, associations, and firms with promotional and other activities.

Food Aid

The United States is the world's leading supplier of food aid. It provides more than half of the global total.

The United States provides food aid mainly through P.L. 480, also known as the Food for Peace Program. Wheat and wheat flour are the main commodities provided as food aid, but rice and vegetable oils are also important in P.L. 480 programs. Higher-value products are made available in special feeding programs. Responsibility for implementing food aid programs is shared by USDA and the U.S. Agency for International Development (AID).

P.L. 480 food aid is provided on concessional terms (Title I) and as donations (Titles II and III). Title I food aid is intended to help develop overseas markets; Titles II and III are for humanitarian or developmental purposes.

Two other food aid programs are conducted under Section 416(b) of the Agricultural Act of 1949 and the Food for Progress Act of 1985. The former provides surplus CCC inventories as donations; the latter provides concessional credit terms or commodity donations to support emerging democracies or countries making free market economic reforms. A recently enacted food aid program, the McGovern-Dole School Food for Education Program, finances school feeding and child nutrition projects in poor countries.

End Notes

[1] OECD countries include Australia, Canada, the European Union, Iceland, Japan, Korea, New Zealand, Norway, Switzerland, Turkey, and the United States.

[2] A tariff quota is defined by WTO as a trade measure applied at the border where quantities inside a quota are charged lower import duty rates than those outside (which can be high).

[3] WTO, *Trade Policy Review: United States 2008*, pp. 81-82, available at http://www.wto.org/english/tratop_e/tpr_e/ tp_rep_e.htm#bycountry.

[4] Ibid, p. 81.

[5] Wheat and wheat flour, coarse grains, rice, vegetable oils, butter and butter oil, skim milk powder, cheese, other milk products, bovine meat, pigmeat, poultry meat, live dairy cattle, and eggs.

In: United States Agricultural Trade
Eds: T. E. Brooks and E. M. Sanders

ISBN: 978-1-61209-128-0
© 2011 Nova Science Publishers, Inc.

Chapter 2

U.S. AGRICULTURAL TRADE BOOSTS OVERALL ECONOMY

William Edmondson

ABSTRACT

U.S. agricultural trade generates employment, income, and purchasing power in both the farm and nonfarm sectors. Each farm export dollar earned stimulated another $1.65 in business activity in calendar year 2006. The $71.0 billion of agricultural exports in 2006 produced an additional $117.2 billion in economic activity for a total economic output of $188.2 billion. Agricultural exports also generated 841,000 full-time civilian jobs, which include 482,000 jobs in the nonfarm sector. Farmers' purchases of fuel, fertilizer, and other inputs to produce commodities for export spurred economic activity in the manufacturing, trade, and transportation sectors.

Keywords: agricultural trade, exports, imports, U.S. farm sector, multipliers, output, employment, income, food processing, bulk, nonbulk

INTRODUCTION

As the world becomes more integrated, global trade and the economic links between countries grow ever stronger. U.S. agricultural trade[1] is a significant contributor to the overall U.S. economy and to the rest of the world's economies. The United States continues to be a net exporter of agricultural products, the surplus helping to offset some of the U.S. nonfarm trade deficit. Trade agreements have expanded agricultural trade and, in turn, have opened the U.S. market to exporting opportunities for both developed and developing countries. Such trade benefits developing countries that in the past have had little market access. Agricultural exports by the United States are now enjoying a resurgence due to rising food demand in emerging markets, reduced competition in feed-grain markets, and a weakened dollar. At the same time the value of agricultural imports is rising, averaging 10-percent growth per year since 2001.

The U.S. farm and rural economies have always been affected by international and domestic macroeconomic trade influences. From early colonial days, when tobacco and cotton were the most important export commodities, to today's grain, oilseed, and processed foods, agricultural trade has been an important part of the U.S. economic engine. The North American Free Trade Agreement (NAFTA) and other bilateral and multilateral trade agreements lowered trade barriers and created additional consumer demand for U.S. agricultural commodities in foreign nations. In turn, that demand is satisfied with purchasing power acquired when their products are sold in the United States and elsewhere. The weakening U.S. dollar, which has now fallen to a 30-year low compared with the world's other major currencies, makes the price of U.S. goods increasingly competitive abroad. Canada and Mexico are the leading U.S. trading partners—together, those nations buy over 35 percent of U.S. exports. Meanwhile, U.S. imports of agricultural goods have not slowed despite the weakened buying power of the U.S. dollar. U.S. consumers continue to demand a large variety of imported goods and are willing to pay a premium for them.

Agricultural trade is most importantly a generator of output, employment, and income in the U.S. economy. For every dollar spent on exports in 2006, another $1.65 was created in the economy to support the exporting activity (see table 1). ERS model results show that every $1 billion of agricultural exports in 2006 requires 11,800 American jobs (see, "Data Sources").

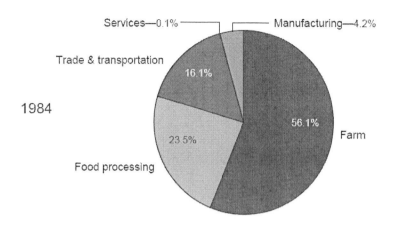

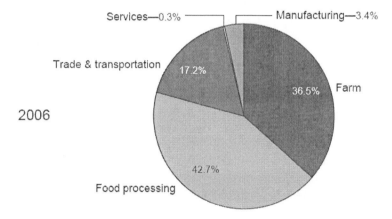

Source: Analysis by Economic Research Service, USDA, based on U.S. Census Bureau trade data, using Bureau of Economic Analysis input-output methodology.

Figure 1. Value share of commodity composition of agricultural exports

HISTORICAL IMPACTS OF TRADE

The impacts of agricultural trade on the U.S. economy change from year to year. The changes have been dramatic since this analysis was first performed in the early 1980s. The changes have occurred because of overall changes to the structure of the U.S. economy and because of changes in the types of commodities exported in the intervening years. As can be seen from figure 1, the industrial sectors' shares of the value of agricultural exports have changed considerably since 1984. The farm sector's 56-percent share in 1984 had shrunk to 36.5 percent in 2006. The food-processing sector's exports increased from 23.5 percent in 1984 to 42.7 percent in 2006. While the shares and values of agricultural exports from sectors fluctuate from year to year, the long-term trend is away from bulk and raw farm exports and toward more processed-product exports.

Just as important as who contributes to the value of agricultural trade is who receives the income derived from those exports. Much depends on the year-to-year commodity composition of the "basket "of goods exported, but some overall trends can be discerned. U.S. farms' 33.1-percent share of export income shrank to 23.8 percent between 1984 and 2006 and the food-processing sector's 14.1 percent fell to 9.7 percent (see figure 2). By contrast, the services sector's share of income more than doubled from 17.2 percent to 35.4 percent. Just as the service sector has become the largest producing sector of the total U.S. economy, it has become the largest earner of income related to agricultural exports. The sector includes data processing as well as financial, legal, managerial, administrative, and many other types of services needed to facilitate the movement of export commodities.

Employment generated by agricultural exports follows the same general trends as do the values of economic activity related to agricultural trade (figure 3 and figure 4) with peaks in the early 1990s and 2000s and valleys midway between. But the jobs-required trend (the types of jobs needed to facilitate the export of agricultural commodities) is more volatile. This volatility occurs because job requirements change with the commodity composition of the exports. For example, most high-value and processed products require more total labor than do raw farm products. This means that in years when nonbulk commodities, composed of high-value products (HVPs) and other types of products that require special handling, are the major share of the "export basket," jobs generated by exports are higher. Some years the opposite holds true. When farm prices are especially low, customers are buying large amounts of bulk grains and oilseeds. Many jobs are created on the farm and in the supporting transportation and distribution industries, but job growth bypasses the processing and manufacturing sectors. In 2006, farm prices were low and the value of bulk exports was low. However, the volume of exports, which determines labor requirements, was high. Because of this, bulk products generated more jobs per dollar in 2006, but nonbulk products generated more of the total share of employment.

U.S. Agricultural Trade Boosts Overall Economy

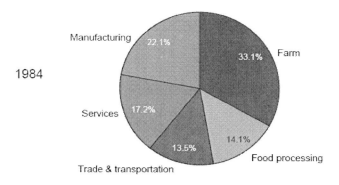

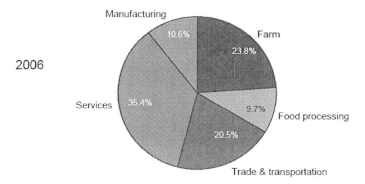

Source: Analysis by Economic Research Service, USDA, based on U.S. Census Bureau trade data, using Bureau of Economic Analysis input-output methodology.

Figure 2. Distribution of income returned for agricultural exports

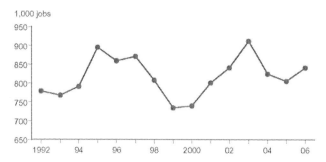

Source: Analysis by Economic Research Service, USDA, based on U.S. Census Bureau trade data, using Bureau of Economic Analysis input-output methodology.

Figure 3. Number of civilian jobs generated by U.S. agricultural exports, 1992-2006

Data Sources

The Bureau of Economic Analysis (BEA), U.S. Department of Commerce, releases a Benchmark Input/Output (I/O) table every 5 years. The benchmark table is at the most highly disaggregated level of over 500 industry sectors. BEA also releases yearly updates to its benchmark table, aggregating those industries to the 79-sectors level. This analysis uses the benchmark table as its starting point because the annually updated tables are aggregated to contain only two agricultural sectors and one food-processing sector. Even though the data for beginning points are older, using the benchmark tables allows analysis of supporting agricultural activity and links to the rest of the economy. Then, the ERS model endogenously updates the information derived from the benchmark that is contained in its models, resulting in a view of the disaggregated agricultural economy that reflects current economic conditions.

Figure 4 shows the historical trends of both direct exports and the indirect supporting activity, i.e., the additional economic activity that it takes to deliver these goods to their final consumer throughout the rest of the economy. Most of this activity falls outside of the farm sector. The largest gap between direct exports and supporting activity occurs in 2006, meaning that agricultural exports generated more additional domestic activity in 2006 than at any other point since 1992.

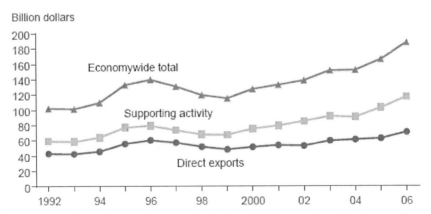

Source: Analysis by Economic Research Service, USDA, based on U.S. Census Bureau trade data, using Bureau of Economic Analysis input-output methodology.

Figure 4. Value of economic activity generated by U.S. agricultural exports, 1992-2006
Billion dollars

THE IMPACT OF AGRICULTURAL TRADE, 2006

In calendar year 2006, the $71.0 billion of agricultural exports produced an additional $117.2 billion in economic activity for a total of $188.2 billion of economic output. Supporting activity continued to climb after surpassing the $100 billion mark for the first time in 2005. Agricultural exports also generated 841,000 full-time civilian jobs, including 482,000 jobs in the nonfarm sector. Farmers' purchases of fuel, fertilizer, and other inputs to produce commodities for export spurred economic activity in the manufacturing, trade, and transportation sectors.

The production equivalent from almost one-fourth of U.S. cropland moved into export channels in 2006. Of raw crops, the United States exported 49 percent of food grain production, 16 percent of feed grains, and more than 38 percent of oilseeds. While the percentage of production of food-grain exports held steady and that of feed-grain exports decreased, oilseed exports increased significantly over 2005. Because exports increased more than imports, net agricultural exports in 2006 contributed $5.7 billion to the overall U.S. economy, $2.1 billion more than in 2005 ($3.6 billion).

It is not currently possible to measure the total economic activity associated with imports because there are no end-use data on imports available. After imports enter the United States and their value is recorded at that stage, imports are no longer tracked as imports. They then mix in the general domestic economy to be used in the same fashion as domestically produced goods. The end-use of a product is what determines its multiplier effects. Imports can be put into inventory (an almost negligible multiplier) and/or used in the most highly processed product (a very large multiplier). There is no feasible way to measure the indirect or supporting impacts of actual agricultural imports in terms of output, employment, value-added or in a multiplier analysis. Only the value of imports as measured upon entry into the U.S. can be discerned (direct effects). Imports can be assigned the generally held view of an economy-wide domestic business multiplier of 2.50, because activities associated with "absorbed" imports are the same as those associated with any other domestic commodity.

To illustrate the point, consider that almost all fishing products are imported. If statistics on consumers' demand and consumption of fish were analyzed, the supporting activity required to deliver that imported fish to the table could be measured. But this would not be the only contribution of fish imports as human food to the economy because the contributions of fish meal and feeds, processed products, and any other uses of fish have not been measured. These uses are completely intertwined with domestic production and to correctly measure these outputs, one would also have to separate the movement of imported fish products from the growing amount of products from domestic farm-raised fish.

The description of economic impacts of imports that follows is not the measurable economic activity associated with exports contrasted to the incalculable supporting activity of imports. Instead, the value of an imported product is estimated as if it were produced in the U.S., and assigned the value of that activity as a theoretical loss of economic activity to the United States.

Commodities come in various forms, including the raw commodity, and do provide employment and income to the economy once they reach our shores. However, once the product is here, it is processed and commingled with other product so that we cannot follow it past the shipping docks. The only actual "loss" to the U.S. economy that can be measured is the actual value of agricultural imports. After the imported product is absorbed into the U.S. economy, the supporting activity required to deliver the imported goods to final consumers is estimated using a general business multiplier "gain" of at least 2.50 (see, "Multipliers").

MULTIPLIERS

An output multiplier is a summation of the effects of $1 of demand for a particular commodity from a particular industry. In this paper, demand is for agricultural exports. The employment multipliers are expressed in terms of jobs per billion dollars of agricultural exports. These multipliers measure the direct and indirect effects of an economic activity (exports) by weighing the impacts of sales and purchases between all goods and service sectors of the economy; sales to final demand (consumption, investment, government, and net exports); and purchases of land, labor, and capital services. Multipliers are best suited to describe activity that has already taken place in an economy and can be measured. It would be inappropriate to use these multipliers to forecast the economic impacts of future trade. Multipliers also describe, when dissected to their component parts, the interrelatedness of sectors in a base period.

The multiplier of 1.65 reported here represents the additional supporting activity generated by the original $1 purchase of agricultural exports. They are sometimes combined in popular parlance and expressed as a total, so that the agricultural exports multiplier becomes 2.65. There is a generally held view of an economywide business multiplier of 2.50. Therefore, agricultural exports generate more output in the economy than do most other domestic industries. The estimated employment multiplier for 2006 was close to 12,000 jobs per billion dollars of agricultural exports. Job requirements vary greatly across industries.

EXPORTS GENERATE NEW BUSINESS, ADD JOBS

Of the $71 billion in direct U.S. agricultural exports in 2006, the value of exported raw products was $25.9 billion, compared with $30.3 billion of processed commodities, and $14.8 billion for transport and trade services. There was $117.2 billion of supporting or indirect activity generated by agricultural exports in 2006 that encompasses the value of activity required to facilitate the movement of exports to their final destination (e.g., computer and financial services, warehousing and distribution, packaging and additional processing). The service sector receives the lion's share of the additional activity, generating $46.9 billion of the $117.2 billion total. All nonfarm sectors of the economy received about 83 percent of this additional economic activity.

Employment required to produce, transport, and service agricultural exports in 2006 increased from 2005 levels. Export commodity mix, price changes, and the volume of goods exported contributed to the rise. Of the 841,000 full-time civilian jobs related to agricultural exports in 2006, more than 359,000 were U.S. farmworkers, an increase of 8,000 jobs in 2006 from 2005. Based on a Bureau of Labor Statistics estimate of 2,206,000 full-time-equivalent agricultural workers, this would mean that approximately 16 percent of the U.S. farm workforce is producing for export. Almost, 482,000 jobs in the nonfarm sector were involved in assembling, processing, distributing, and servicing agricultural products for export. About 65,000 of those were in food processing, 139,000 in trade and transportation, 56,000 in other manufacturing sectors, and 222,000 in other services.

Each dollar of bulk exports has a smaller proportional effect on the nonfarm economy than a dollar of processed, or high-value, exports. Bulk exports of $24.4 billion generated an additional $38.8 billion of business activity while nonbulk exports of $46.6 billion generated $78.4 billion (i.e., $1.59 additional output per dollar of bulk exports, $1.68 for nonbulk exports, and $1.65 for all agricultural exports). Over 50 percent of the additional business activity attributed to bulk exports took place in the service sector and 1 percent in food processing. By contrast, the additional business activity for nonbulk exports was 8 percent in food processing and 34 percent in services (see figures 5, 6, and 7). Of the 841,000 jobs related to U.S. agricultural exports, 490,000 (57 percent) supported nonbulk exports.

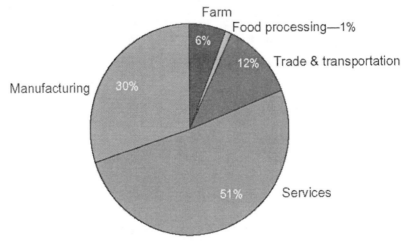

Source: Analysis by Economic Research Service, USDA, based on U.S. Census Bureau trade data, using Bureau of Economic Analysis input-output methodology.

Figure 5. Bulk agricultural exports, 2006, distribution of supporting activity

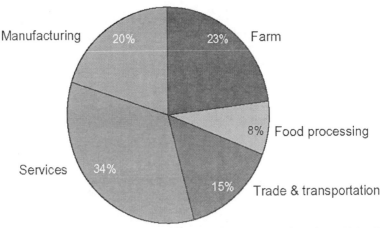

Source: Analysis by Economic Research Service, USDA, based on U.S. Census Bureau trade data, using Bureau of Economic Analysis input-output methodology.

Figure 6. Nonbulk agricultural exports, 2006, distribution of supporting activity

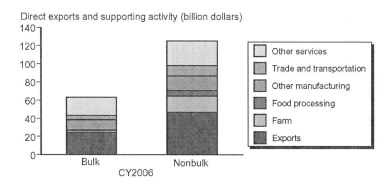

Source: Analysis by Economic Research Service, USDA, based on U.S. Census Bureau trade data, using Bureau of Economic Analysis input-output methodology.

Figure 7. Nonbulk agricultural exports generate more total business activity than bulk

IMPACTS OF AGRICULTURAL IMPORTS ON U.S. OUTPUT

The domestic output effect of the $65.3 billion of agricultural imports into the U.S. in 2006 was $162.2 billion. Just as with exports, moving imported products to consumers generates jobs in the data processing, financial, legal, management, administrative, and marketing sectors. Each dollar spent on imports would have required another $1.48 in supporting goods and services if those imported items had been produced domestically, indicating an output multiplier of 2.48.

When valuing output associated with imports on the U.S. economy, we calculate a theoretical loss of economic activity from imports equal to the value of the product if it were to be produced here. Many imports such as coffee, bananas, and cocoa, have few if any counterparts in U.S. agricultural production. While the purchase of these imports does represent a loss in income to the U.S. economy equivalent to their value at the border, they do not a represent a loss in production or supporting activities.

U.S. agricultural trade has a positive effect on most sectors of the economy. The farm sector's $45.8 billion of output associated with agricultural exports more than offset the $30.5 billion of farm output implicitly lost because of agricultural imports. The nonfarm sectors, including food processing, gained $10.8 billion in total output, creating about 43,600 jobs and generating $4.7 billion in income. The U.S. economy gained a net $26 billion in output (after the theoretical loss to agricultural imports is considered). Outside of farming and food processing, the United States theoretically lost a net $2.6 billion from direct agricultural trade, that is, exports minus imports of agricultural goods that are neither farm nor processed goods, but gained $14.3 billion in total output because the direct plus indirect value of these exports was greater than that of the imports. Although there were imports of nonfarm, nonfood- processing of greater value than exports in 2006, the U.S. exports of this category generated more total output than imports did in the economy.

METHODOLOGY APPENDIX

These estimates of the economic activities associated with exports are derived from the *1997 Benchmark Input-Output Accounts*, maintained by the U.S. Department of Commerce's Bureau of Economic Analysis. The economic methodology used to make specific estimates of the impacts of 2006 agricultural trade is given here.

Employment, output, and/or income related to exports of agricultural commodities can be estimated when an input/output (I/O) transaction table is available. Benchmark tables are available every 5 years, with a 5-year lag. Updates at the aggregate level are produced every year, with a 2-year lag. A 2002 benchmark table is being prepared for analysis.

Income Generation

Since income (or gross domestic product) measures, in an aggregated form, the sum of value added in various I/O sectors, then

$$\text{Output} = \sum_{j=1}^{n} X$$

$$\text{Income} = \sum_{j=1}^{n} V_j \quad (1)$$

where V_j is value added in sector j. Under an I/O structure, value added is a fixed proportion of output, so that income can be written in a matrix form as:

$$\text{Output} = X = (I-A)^{-1} F \tag{2}$$

Income = $Y = vX = v(I-A)^{-1} F$

Where X = an n x 1 vector of sector outputs

$(I-A)^{-1}$ = an n x n I/O total requirements matrix

F = an n x 1 vector of final demand for agricultural exports

Y = an n x 1 vector of income originating from each sector of the economy due to agricultural exports

v = an n x n diagonal matrix of value added per dollar of sector output coefficients

Employment Generation

Using the above notations, employment in each sector of I/O industries is derived as:

$$E = L(I-A)^{-1} F \tag{3}$$

Where $(I-A)^{-1}$ and F are as previously defined

L = an n x n diagonal matrix of civilian employment coefficients per dollar of sector output

E = an n x 1 vector of sector employment needs related to the level of agricultural exports defined in vector F

Nonbase Year Estimation

To estimate output, income, and employment multipliers related to exports for years beyond the published I/O tables, one must work with less information because current year $(I-A)^{-1}$, v, and L are unavailable. Yet, there are observable changes that can be incorporated into the analysis, such as changes in labor productivity and in the sectoral composition of final demand. Changes in the composition of final demand may also require changes in industry output requirements, which, in turn, change interindustry demand. Likewise, increases in labor productivity imply that the same output can be produced with a smaller workforce or that more output can be produced with the same size workforce.

Changes in the yearly commodity composition of agricultural exports are available from the Foreign Agricultural Trade of the United States (FATUS) summary tables. Available at: http://www.ers.usda.gov/Data/FATUS/ Monthly Summary.htm.

Nonbase year income is estimated through a modification of equation 2.

$$Y = qT \qquad (4)$$

Where $T = v(I-A)^{-1} F'$
q = an n x n diagonal matrix of output originating price deflators
F' = an n x 1 vector of current year exports
Nonbase year employment is estimated through a modification of equation 3.

Labor productivity changes in farming and in nonfarm sectors are available from USDA and the U.S. Department of Labor, respectively. Therefore, equation (3) is modified to incorporate the effect of productivity change in the generation of employment.

$$E = pW \qquad (5)$$

Where p = an n x n diagonal matrix showing the ratio of base year labor productivity to current year productivity and

$$W = L(I-A)^{-1} F'$$

Table 1. U.S. economic activity triggered by agricultural trade, 2006

Item	2004 Total	2005 Total	2006 Total	2006 Bulk	2006 Nonbulk
			Billion dollars		
Economic activity generated by agricultural exports	152.2	166.1	188.2	63.2	125.0
Farm	39.8	39.6	45.8	21.3	24.5
Food processing	29.8	33.2	37.0	0.3	36.7
Other manufacturing	23.0	26.4	29.8	11.5	18.3
Trade and transportation	23.4	24.9	28.5	10.2	18.3
Other services	36.2	41.9	47.1	20.0	27.1
Exports	61.4	62.9	71.0	24.4	46.6
Agricultural imports	52.6	59.3	65.3	15.6	49.7
Agricultural trade balance	8.8	3.6	5.7	8.8	-3.1
Supporting activities	90.8	103.2	117.2	38.8	78.4
Farm	15.9	16.8	19.9	2.3	17.6
Food processing	5.5	6.0	6.7	0.3	6.4
Other manufacturing	20.8	24.2	27.4	11.5	15.9
Trade and transportation		12.7	14.3	16.3	4.8	11.5

Other services	36.1	41.7	46.9	20.0	26.9
Percent					
Nonfarm share of supporting economic activity	83	84	83	94	77
Export multiplier (additional business activity generated by $1 of exports)	1.48	1.64	1.65	1.59	1.68
1,000 jobs					
Employment generated by agricultural exports	825	806	841	351	490
Farm	388	351	359	180	179
Nonfarm	437	455	482	171	311
Food processing	58	62	65	0	65
Other manufacturing	54	54	56	19	37
Trade and transportation	129	130	139	50	89
Other services	196	209	222	101	121
Employment per billion dollars of agricultural exports	13.4	12.8	11.8	14.4	10.5
Percent					
Share of farm workforce supported by agricultural exports	17	16	16	8	8
Domestic equivalent of economic activity generated by agricultural imports	127.3	145.3	162.0	3.8	158.2
Farm	24.9	27.4	30.5	1.4	29.1
Food processing	33.5	37.1	40.6	0.0	40.6
Other manufacturing	19.9	23.6	26.6	0.7	25.9
Trade and transportation	19.7	22.5	25.0	0.6	24.4
Other services	29.2	34.5	39.3	1.1	38.2
Net domestic equivalent of total output gain or loss to agricultural imports	24.9	20.8	26.2	59.4	-33.2
Farm	14.9	12.2	15.3	19.9	-4.6
Food processing	3.7	-3.9	-3.6	0.3	-3.9
Other manufacturing	3.1	2.8	3.2	10.8	-7.6
Trade and transportation	3.7	2.4	3.5	9.6	-6.1
Other services	7.0	7.4	7.8	18.9	-11.1
Nonfarm, nonfood processing sectors:					
Net direct benefit from exports	-0.8	-2.6	-2.6	5.1	-7.7

Table 1 (Continued)

Item	2004 Total	2005 Total	2006 Total	2006 Bulk	2006 Nonbulk
Net increased output from exports	14.6	15.1	16.9	34.2	-17.3
Percent					
Farm share of total income from exports	26	23	24	33	18
Trade and transportation share of total income from exports	21	21	21	19	22

Source: USDA, Economic Research Service.

REFERENCES

[1] Edmondson, W., Somwaru, A. & Petrulis, M. (1995). *Measuring the Economywide Effect of the Farm Sector*, Technical Bulletin, *1843*, July.
[2] Miller, Ronald, E. & Peter, D. (1985). Blair. *Input-output Analysis: Foundations and Extensions*, Prentice Hall, Inc., Englewood Cliffs, NJ,.
[3] Schluter, G. & Edmondson, W. (1994). *USDA's Agricultural Trade Multipliers—A Primer*, Agricultural Information Bulletin, *697*, April.
[4] U.S. Department of Commerce, Bureau of Economic Analysis. (2002). *Survey of Current Business: Benchmark Input and Output Accounts of the United States, 1997*, December.
[5] U.S. Department of Labor, Bureau of Labor Statistics. (2007). *Monthly Labor Review*, September.

End Notes

[1] ERS has data on agricultural trade flows in its U.S. Agricultural Trade briefing room. See http://www.ers.usda.gov/Briefing/AgTrade/.

In: United States Agricultural Trade
Eds: T. E. Brooks and E. M. Sanders

ISBN: 978-1-61209-128-0
© 2011 Nova Science Publishers, Inc.

Chapter 3

GLOBAL GROWTH, MACROECONOMIC CHANGE, AND U.S. AGRICULTURAL TRADE

Mark Gehlhar, Erik Dohlman, Nora Brooks, Alberto Jerardo and Thomas Vollrath

ABSTRACT

After a decade of uneven export growth and rapidly growing imports, U.S. agriculture has begun to reassert its position in global trade markets. Rising exports and signs of moderating demand for imports mark a departure from previous trends. This report places past trends and emerging developments in perspective by spotlighting the role of two specific factors that help steer U.S. agricultural trade patterns: global growth and shifts in foreign economic activity that affect U.S. exports, and macroeconomic factors underlying the growth of U.S. imports. Consistent with actual changes in the level and destination of U.S. exports, model simulations corroborate the contention that renewed export growth can be sustained by expanding incomes and growing food import demand in emerging economies. In contrast, the rapid growth of U.S. agricultural imports appears less related to domestic income growth than to changing consumer preferences and other, perhaps less sustainable, macroeconomic conditions that fostered the growth of U.S. current account deficits.

Keywords: agricultural trade, trade balance, income growth, economic development, population, macroeconomics, exchange rates, current account, growth projections.

ACKNOWLEDGMENTS

The authors thank the following individuals for their valuable insights and recommendations: Barry Krissoff, Suchada Langley, Bill Liefert, Daniel Pick, Mathew Shane, Paul Sundell, and Paul Westcott of USDA, Economic Research Service. We also thank Ernest Carter, USDA, Foreign Agricultural Service; Catherine Mann of the Peterson Institute for International Economics and Brandeis University; and Jeffrey Reimer of Oregon State University for their helpful suggestions. The authors also thank John Weber and Anne Pearl for editorial and design assistance.

SUMMARY

Historically, U.S. agricultural exports have been highly erratic, with brief periods of strong growth to individual markets often followed by interludes of reduced demand. The growth of U.S. agricultural imports has been comparatively steady and, in recent years, increasingly strong. After peaking at a record $27 billion in 1996, the U.S. agricultural trade surplus dropped below $5 billion a decade later, due to a temporary downturn in export growth and fast-rising imports. More recently, however, rising exports to a broader spectrum of countries and strong but moderating demand for imports appear to signal a reversal of past trends. Many different factors, particularly differences in foreign economic growth rates in key markets and macroeconomic forces, are altering the course of U.S. agricultural trade.

What is the Issue?

In previous decades, U.S. agricultural export growth relied heavily on demand from key high-income markets, such as Japan and the European Union. In the absence of significant new openings in market access, limited economic growth and stagnant food demand in these markets contributed to a decline in their importance as a destination for U.S. exports—placing a drag on overall U.S. export growth. Currently, however, increased demand from fast-growing emerging markets is offsetting weaker growth elsewhere, leading to upward revisions in USDA's long-term export projections. Also, the unprecedented recent growth of U.S. agricultural imports is far more rapid than what would have been expected based on domestic income and population growth rates. Is the simultaneous growth of exports and imports a temporary trend, or one that will be sustained? Previous periods of strong growth have rarely been sustained for more than a few years at a time. Clarifying the influence of foreign economic growth and macroeconomic forces on export and import growth may enable stakeholders to gauge the future direction of U.S. agricultural trade.

What did the Study Find?

Income levels and the rate of economic growth are key determinants of foreign demand for U.S. agricultural exports, and differences between developed-country and emerging-market growth have played a strong role in shaping U.S. export patterns. Slow income and population growth in traditionally important high-income markets, and a low propensity for consumers in these countries to spend additional income on food, have curtailed U.S. exports to these areas since the mid-1990s. New demand from emerging markets, however, is more than offsetting weakened demand elsewhere. These markets provide a foundation for sustained growth of U.S. exports, which in FY 2008 are on track for a fifth consecutive year of record demand.

Rising incomes in emerging markets, in conjunction with a high tendency for consumers in these areas to spend their additional income on food, helped spur a 50-percent increase in global agricultural trade in just 5 years (2001-05). The impact on U.S. agricultural exports is becoming more appreciable as emerging markets continue to raise their share of world trade. In the early 1990s, emerging markets accounted for just 30 percent of U.S. exports, but steady economic growth and continued population gains have raised their share to 43 percent. In 2006, China and Mexico combined accounted for 25 percent of total U.S. agricultural exports—nearly triple their share in 1990.

The shift in the direction of trade from mature economies to emerging markets potentially signals continued strong foreign demand for U.S. exports in the future. Based on analysis of global economic growth and population changes, these factors accounted for U.S. export growth of 2.6 percent annually during 1990-2001 but are anticipated to contribute to a projected 3.7-percent annual growth during 2006-16. Accordingly, emerging markets would account for nearly 60 percent of U.S. agricultural exports within a decade.

In contrast to exports, domestic population growth and economic growth do not appear to have been the primary drivers of U.S. import demand during the past decade. U.S. agricultural imports have doubled since 1996, with average import growth surpassing 10 percent annually since 2001. Two independent factors have helped to contribute to U.S. import growth: consumer preferences for product variety; and, equally important, broad macroeconomic conditions that fostered the growth of the U.S. current account deficit. The current account measures the balance of trade in goods and services and net investment earnings to and from the rest of the world. Supported by increased wealth, declining domestic savings, and a relatively resilient dollar, the U.S. current account deficit has been rising steadily, reaching a record $880 billion (6.3 percent of GDP) in 2006.

Because current account deficits represent the level of foreign lending to the United States, foreign investment and savings decisions increasingly influence economic variables that determine export and import demand. Reduced foreign demand for U.S. financial assets, for example, can cause higher interest rates, a weaker dollar, subdued domestic consumption growth, and higher net agricultural exports. Although there is no consensus, many analysts consider such an adjustment likely. Alternatively, U.S. consumption and the value of the dollar could remain steady, supporting continued robust growth of agricultural imports.

How was the Study Conducted?

To distinguish between the impacts of global growth factors and other macroeconomic influences on agricultural trade, two separate economic models were employed. Global economic growth and population impacts on world and U.S. trade were evaluated with growth simulations using a static global modeling framework (GTAP). This model generates growth-related effects on past and future U.S. and world trade and illustrates how they contributed to the previous slowdown and current expansion of U.S. agricultural export growth. This framework does not address macroeconomic factors affecting exchange rates or international financial flows. A separate dynamic model of the U.S. economy (USAGE) was used to examine alternative macroeconomic conditions related to exchange rates and changes in foreign demand for U.S. financial assets. The main scenario centers on the implications of changing demand for U.S. financial assets by foreigners. The model was used to trace the effects of resulting exchange rate and other macroeconomic changes on domestic consumption and agricultural trade.

INTRODUCTION

In the past several decades, U.S. agriculture has often faced volatile swings in demand for its exports, while U.S. import growth has been comparatively steady, even becoming increasingly strong in recent years. Following a record $27 billion agricultural trade surplus in 1996, for example, U.S. export values temporarily declined, while import growth continued unabated. In 2006, the agricultural trade surplus dipped below $5 billion (see appendix A), but rising U.S. exports and signs of moderating import demand now stand in marked contrast to previous trends. U.S. agricultural exports in fiscal year (FY) 2008 are expected to reach a fifth consecutive year of record shipments, and U.S. import growth, while still strong, is at its slowest pace since 2003 (figure 1). Many different factors—ranging from shifting consumer preferences to trade policy changes—affect U.S. agricultural trade. This study highlights two specific factors instrumental in determining U.S. export and import trends in recent years:

- *Structural shifts in global growth* and foreign economic activity, which primarily affect U.S. agricultural exports; and
- *Macroeconomic conditions* that guide broader changes in the U.S. trade and current account position, which have strongly influenced U.S. agricultural imports.

The term "structural shifts" refers to differences in economic development stages and food import demand between high-income and emerging markets, and their influence on the overall level and pattern of U.S. agricultural exports. The analysis of macroeconomic conditions focuses specifically on the causes of U.S. current account deficits, potential changes that may place downward pressure on the U.S. dollar, and the impact of these conditions on agricultural trade.[1] These factors are important, not just for understanding past trade patterns, but also for providing insights to future implications for U.S. trade.

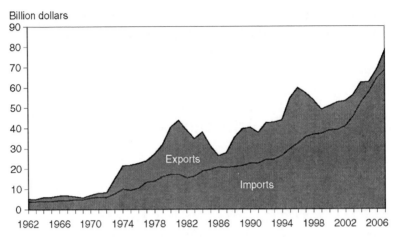

Source: Prepared by USDA, ERS using data from U.S. Department of Commerce, Bureau of the Census.

Figure 1. U.S. agricultural imports rise steadily, while exports are more volatile

Income, population, and the rate of economic growth in importing countries have long been recognized as key determinants of foreign demand for U.S. agricultural products. Many analysts (USDA, 1996) anticipated sustained rapid growth in exports throughout the 1990s, for example, based largely on increased demand from fast-growing emerging markets.[2] However, analysts did not foresee a decline in demand from high-income markets. In Japan and the European Union (EU), relatively slow growth in income and population helped induce a drop in demand for U.S. food products. In 1996, these two markets accounted for $21 billion (35 percent) of U.S. agricultural exports, but by 2006, the total was less than $15.3 billion (22 percent). A low propensity for consumers to spend additional income on food, aging populations (with reduced dietary needs), and, until 2002, an appreciating dollar also contributed to dampening export demand.

Today U.S. agricultural exports are once again entering a period of rapid growth, marked by 5 consecutive years of record shipments (FY 2004-08).[3] In contrast to the past, new demand from emerging markets is more than compensating for weakened demand elsewhere. Rising incomes, in conjunction with a high propensity for consumers to spend that income on food, have helped spur a 50-percent increase in global food trade in just 5 years (2001-05). During the entire preceding decade, global agricultural trade expanded less than 25 percent. Representing a major departure from past trends, export demand now appears to be firmly supported by markets that are experiencing strong growth in Gross Domestic Product (GDP) and spending relatively large shares of income on food. U.S. exports in FY 2007 are at a record $78 billion, up more than $24 billion from 5 years earlier. USDA has raised its 10-year projection of U.S. agricultural exports from $84 billion (in 2015) to $93 billion (USDA, 2006; USDA, February 2007).

In contrast to factors influencing demand for U.S. exports, domestic population growth and economic growth do not appear to have been the primary drivers of U.S. import demand during the past decade. U.S. agricultural imports have doubled since 1996, reaching a record $64 billion in FY 2006. Average import growth has surpassed 10 percent annually since 2001, but projected growth for FY 2007 is at the slowest pace since 2003. While a number of factors underlie the growth of U.S. agricultural imports, the recent surge appears to be connected to the same macroeconomic conditions contributing to the overall growth in merchandise imports and trade deficits. Recent economic literature attributes the growth in U.S. imports to such factors as increased wealth, low domestic savings rates, strong consumption growth, and foreign capital inflows that have kept U.S. interest rates low and the dollar exchange rate relatively strong (Bernanke, 2005). Some observers (e.g., Edwards, 2006) now question whether these factors can persist, raising the possibility that further exchange rate depreciation and other adjustments could eventually reinforce export demand and dampen import growth.

To better understand and distinguish between the impacts of global growth factors and other macroeconomic influences on agricultural trade, this study employs two separate economic models:

- Global economic growth and population impacts on world and U.S. trade are evaluated with growth simulations from a global modeling framework (GTAP). This model illustrates growth-related effects on past and future U.S. and world trade and demonstrates how these factors contributed to the previous slowdown and current expansion of U.S. agricultural exports. This framework does not address macroeconomic factors affecting exchange rates, interest rates, or other variables affecting consumption and trade.
- Alternative macroeconomic conditions related to exchange rates and changes in foreign demand for U.S. financial assets are evaluated with a separate dynamic model of the U.S. economy (USAGE). The main scenario in USAGE centers on the implications of changing demand for U.S. financial assets by foreign investors and traces the effects of

resulting exchange rate and other macroeconomic changes on domestic consumption and agricultural trade.

Neither model explicitly addresses historical changes in trade policy or consumer preferences, but inferences about the influence of these factors can be made based on the model results.

Global Growth, Structural Shifts, and Implications for U.S. Agricultural Exports

Differences in foreign economic growth patterns are statistically one of the strongest factors associated with changes in U.S. agricultural exports (Mattson and Koo, 2005). While overall global food demand generally tracks aggregate population and income growth, changes in world food trade reflect not just the rate of GDP growth in importing countries but also the changing preferences for foreign products and the level of economic development. In recent decades, for example, unstable U.S. export growth in large part stemmed from slowdowns in both income growth and population growth in key U.S. markets, such as Japan and the EU, the leading destinations for U.S. exports for most of the past 40 years. Over the period, these markets experienced modestly rising per capita incomes, but total food consumption and import growth were eventually restrained by limited population growth and the declining propensity for consumers to spend additional income on food, which is characteristic of consumers in high-income countries (Seale, Regmi, and Bernstein, 2003). More recently, however, economic growth in emerging markets has begun to alter global and U.S. agricultural export patterns, contributing to renewed export growth.[4]

A key factor behind the renewed growth of U.S. exports is that demand from emerging markets is finally having an appreciable impact on both global food demand and U.S. exports. Although emerging markets contributed to the growth of global and U.S. food trade throughout the 1990s, gains since 2000 have been far more dramatic. Global agricultural trade expanded less than 25 percent during the 1990s but has already grown 50 percent in the first part of this decade, spurred by rising incomes in emerging markets. As a result, the share of U.S. exports destined for emerging markets climbed from 30 percent during the early 1990s to 43 percent in 2006. Overall, U.S. exports are up from $51 billion in FY 2000 to $78 billion in FY 2007.

This growth is attributed mostly to middle-income countries that are experiencing rapid economic development, such as Mexico and China.[5] These two countries now account for 25 percent of U.S. exports—nearly triple their share in 1990. Structural features of the world economy will continue to affect U.S. agricultural exports in the long term—the next decade and beyond. In some countries, trade liberalization and other economic reforms have reinforced or accelerated trade expansion (in other cases, trade and exchange rate policies have hindered trade), but effects of trade policy are inherently difficult to distinguish from the effects of economic growth and are not explicitly considered in this report (see, "A Historical View of U.S. Agricultural Exports").

A HISTORICAL VIEW OF U.S AGRICULTURAL EXPORTS

Compared with the steady growth of U.S. agricultural imports, the growth of U.S. exports has been volatile, with periods of intermittently strong growth occurring in a succession of developed-country markets: first the European Union (EU), then Japan, and, finally, Canada. Export growth to these markets was often driven by policy-related factors, but the lack of continuity in export growth to these markets (Canada being an exception) is also associated with the slow pace of income and population growth and limited expansion of food consumption (see Mattson and Koo, 2005, for a detailed description of changes in U.S. agricultural exports and imports by region and category).

The EU was the leading market for the United States for more than three decades, but weakening demand and increased domestic supply from the EU—combined with the emergence of the EU's Common Agricultural Policy—contributed to sharply reduced demand for U.S. agricultural products by the mid-1980s. By the late 1980s, the EU's position as the leading market for U.S. exports was supplanted by Japan. Trade liberalization continued to boost U.S. exports to Japan in the early 1990s, but trade to Japan has been declining since 1996, even before the loss of the beef market following the December 2003 discovery in the U.S. of a cow with Bovine Spongiform Encephalopathy (BSE). As with the EU, overall food demand in Japan stagnated due to slowing population growth and lackluster economic conditions.[1] By 2006, the combined share of U.S. exports to the EU and Japan fell to 22 percent—down from 50 percent three decades earlier.

In 2002, Canada replaced Japan as the largest single-country market for U.S. agricultural exports. U.S. export growth to Canada, although remaining strong and steady, is not likely to continue at the same pace as in the past 15 years, when the impacts of the 1989 CAFTA and 1994 NAFTA trade liberalization process unfolded. Import growth in Canada, unlike in other high-income markets, is not driven by income and population-related changes. Instead, trade between the United States and Canada has been driven largely by market integration and the ongoing industry rationalization resulting in increased efficiency in each country's food processing and distribution sectors.

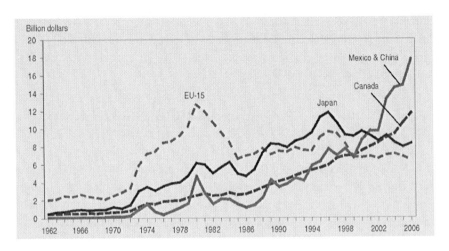

Source: Prepared by USDA, ERS using data from U.S. Department of Commerce, Bureau of the Census.
U.S. agricultural exports to some traditionally important high-income markets have declined
[1] In contrast, U.S. agricultural imports have risen sharply in recent years, exceeding 10 percent growth annually since 2001. But, as detailed later, this pattern is not as closely tied to income or population growth in the United States, so the discussion here focuses on U.S. exports.

Development, Population, and Faster World Growth

Although U.S. exports historically have been quite volatile, there are a number of reasons to believe that the increased prominence of emerging markets in global food trade could lead to periods of sustained export growth. In the past decade, the emerging countries' share of global GDP has risen from 43 percent in 1996 to 50 percent in 2006 (as measured by purchasing power parity), and the emerging countries' share of global trade has climbed at an even faster pace. According to recent growth projections, developing regions, such as China, Southeast Asia, Mexico, Central America, and India, will likely continue to increase their share of global GDP in the coming decades. They will also account for 95 percent of the expected increase of 1 billion persons to the global population by the year 2020.

Because faster growing emerging markets will continue to increase their share of global economic activity, overall world GDP and trade growth is expected to strengthen in the next decade (Global Insight). This growth should continue even as population and GDP growth rates subside in some individual countries. China, other Asia-Pacific countries (excluding Japan), and Latin America are not expected to grow as fast as in the recent past, but GDP and population growth rates are still expected to be relatively strong, especially compared with those in Europe and Japan (figures 2 and 3). Even so, the proportion of U.S. agricultural exports destined for markets with GDPs growing faster than that of the United States has increased steadily, exceeding 55 percent in 2006. Consequently, the increasing prominence of emerging economies in global trade is likely to exert an ongoing influence on the U.S. agricultural sector.[6]

The rapid growth in global agricultural trade also is attributed in part to the dual role played by emerging economies as both exporters and importers. In most developing countries, the share of the population employed in agriculture remains large, and agriculture continues to be a major contributor to GDP growth. As a result, emerging economies with favorable natural resources for agriculture have increasingly become both major exporters and importers of agricultural goods as they specialize in the crop and livestock sectors for which they have a comparative advantage. For example, Mexico's agricultural exports to the United States have been nearly as large as agricultural imports from the United States over the last decade, and China has simultaneously increased exports of labor-intensive horticultural crops and imports of more land and capital-intensive crops, such as oilseeds and cotton. Other countries, such as Brazil and Argentina, have emerged as major agricultural exporters and competitors with the United States in a number of crops (Schnepf, Dohlman, and Bolling, 2001). Consumers in many of the faster growing markets also have diversifying diets that cannot be satisfied by domestic agricultural production alone. As incomes rise, food demand can outgrow domestic production, fueling import demand (Mellor, 1982).

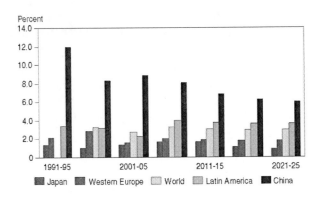

Historical and projected annual GDP growth (5-year average). Data for "world" not available for 1991-95.
Source: Prepared by USDA, ERS using data from Global Insight.

Figure 2. GDP growth in mature markets lags

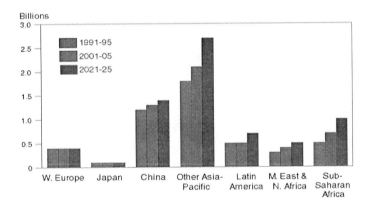

Source: Prepared by USDA, ERS using data from Global Insight.

Figure 3. Population growth is strongest in Asia and Latin America

Sustained Demand and Implications for U.S. Agricultural Exports

In addition to being stimulated by faster overall world growth, food expenditure shares also will factor into sustained growth of agricultural exports. Food purchases represent a much larger share of new expenditures in developing countries than in high-income markets. For example, for every additional dollar of income, consumers in Egypt, Indonesia, and Vietnam spend more than 25 cents on food, whereas consumers in France, Japan, and the United States spend less than 10 cents (USDA, 2002; Regmi, 2001). It will take decades for the developing countries to reach a level of development—characterized by high per capita incomes, a large middle class, and an aging population—where food demand becomes saturated.

The larger proportion of young people in developing countries is another indicator suggesting more sustained demand growth than in the past. Slowing economic growth and food demand is associated with an aging, high-income population, and food demand tends to taper off as the population matures, even while per capita incomes may rise. Less than 15 percent of the population in Japan and Europe is under age 14, in contrast to roughly a third of the population in India and Mexico (table 1). The larger proportion of young people (under age 14) in developing countries favors continued growth in food demand. The impacts of developing-country population and income growth—and associated trends, such as urbanization and a more youthful age structure—broadly correspond to changes in food demand and agricultural trade.

Continued per capita income gains in emerging markets, such as developing Asia and Latin America, have already transformed these regions into increasingly important destinations for U.S. agricultural exports. In the past decade, there has been a pronounced shift in U.S. agricultural export destinations. In 2006, for example, exports to China and Mexico combined exceeded those to the European Union and Japan for the first time (figure 4).

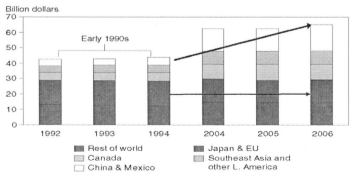

Source: Prepared by USDA, ERS using data from U.S. Department of Commerce, Bureau of the Census.

Figure 4. U.S. exports shifting toward emerging markets

Table 1. Disparities in per capita GDP, imports, and age structure of population, 2004

	Per capita GDP	Per capita agri-imports	Share of population age 65 and above	Share of population age 0-14
	U.S. dollars		Percent	
Japan	38,609	325	19	14
United States	36,655	205	12	20
Canada	24,688	475	13	18
European Union	20,934	200	17	15
Mexico	5,968	129	5	32
China	1,323	19	7	22
India	538	5	5	33
World	5,516	100	7	28

Source: Prepared by USDA, ERS using data from World Bank (2006) and FAO (2006).

Macroeconomic Influences on U.S. Agricultural Trade

In addition to the influence of shifting patterns of growth in foreign populations and per capita income, cyclical macroeconomic factors associated with consumption and savings patterns, interest rates, and exchange rates affect U.S. agricultural trade. Over much of the past decade, for example, conditions in the U.S. economy encouraged strong consumer spending, leading to rapid across- the-board import growth that overwhelmed a more limited expansion of exports. Recent economic evidence suggests that U.S. consumers, encouraged first by stock market appreciation and then by housing sector wealth gains, drew upon their equity, reduced their savings, and spent more on imports and some export-oriented products. At the same time, growing inflows of foreign capital kept interest rates low and the dollar relatively strong.

Although the dollar has depreciated since 2002, making imports more expensive and exports less expensive, U.S. spending has remained strong and contributed to progressively larger trade and current account deficits.[7] In 2006, the U.S. current account deficit amounted to a record $880 billion (6.3 percent of GDP), up from a $100-billion deficit in 1996. This increase largely reflected rapid import growth in all categories of trade—most notably consumer goods and industrial supplies, but also, to a certain extent, traditional "surplus" categories, such as services and foods, feeds, and beverages (figure 5).[8] Declining trade balances in all sectors of the economy indicate that recent changes in U.S. agricultural trade are part of an economy-wide phenomenon.

The high level of the U.S. current account deficit has raised widespread debate about the sustainability of such deficits and the extent to which a potential adjustment would affect U.S. exchange rates, interest rates, consumer spending, and, by extension, food product trade. Different levels of national savings and investment rates can allow countries to be net importers and borrowers over extended periods, but eventually trade (and current account) imbalances are expected to readjust as net importers subsequently "repay" their borrowing with net exports.

Given the importance of foreign capital inflows (lending) to the United States, a central concern is that improved investment prospects elsewhere, or a desire for currency diversification, could reduce the willingness of foreign investors and institutions to hold U.S. financial assets (see, "Understanding the Current Account Balance"). Some of the factors underlying the U.S. current account deficit suggest that an adjustment may occur, having implications for U.S. agricultural trade. Without an increase in rates of return on U.S. assets, lower demand for dollars would lead to further dollar depreciation, more subdued U.S. consumption growth, and lower overall deficits—all of which could raise net U.S. agricultural exports.

Implications of Current Account Deficits

The growth of U.S. current account deficits is linked with both a decline in U.S. savings and changes in investment and savings decisions abroad—particularly among oil exporters and developing countries that have experienced financial crises in the last decade.[9] Savings have flowed to the United States from nonindustrial countries largely because of the attractiveness of secure, but relatively low, returns on U.S. investments—as reflected by the increase in foreign central bank reserves held as U.S. treasury notes.[10] However, the unprecedented size of the U.S. deficit and the source of lending to the United States each suggest that adjustments could take place that will eventually boost U.S. exports and dampen import growth in all sectors of the economy, including agriculture.

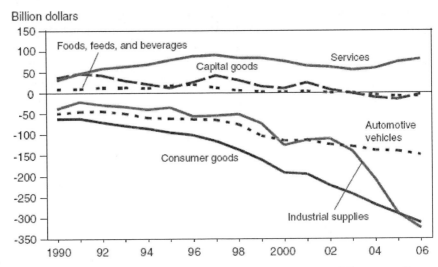

Source: Prepared by USDA, ERS using data from U.S. Department of Commerce, Bureau of the Census.

Figure 5. U.S. trade balance declines in all categories

At the end of the 1990s (when the U.S. current account deficit was equivalent to about 3 percent of GDP), Mann (1999) suggested that the current account deficit was sustainable at that time because of the dollar's special position as the "numeraire" (international reserve) currency in international financial markets. However, Mann noted that as long as the U.S. economy continued to grow faster than that of the rest of the world, foreign investors would continue to choose U.S. dollar denominated assets, keeping the dollar high and ultimately raising the chances of a more profound shift in investor sentiment leading to dollar depreciation. More recently, the Organisation for Economic Co-operation and Development's U.S. Economic Survey (2004) concluded that an adjustment in the U.S. current account may eventually be precipitated by a change in U.S. and global demand for U.S. dollar assets because "at some stage, these assets may come to occupy too large a share of foreign portfolios, even though their relative returns remain favorable."[11]

One reason to believe that capital inflows to the United States eventually may subside is that the less-developed economies accounting for a large share of foreign lending to the U.S normally would attract, or borrow, financial capital rather than lending as their current account surpluses indicate. According to conventional economic theory, the less-advanced economies typically would offer higher (but riskier) rates of return on investment because capital in those countries is relatively scarce. Bernanke (2005) observes: We see that many of the major industrial countries—particularly Japan and some countries in Western Europe—have both strong reasons to save (to help support future retirees) and increasingly limit ed investment opportunities at home (because workforces are shrinking and capital-labor ratios are already high). In contrast, most developing countries have younger and more rapidly growing workforces, as well as relatively low ratios of capital to labor, conditions that imply that the returns to capital in those countries may potentially be quite high. Basic economic logic thus suggests that, in the longer term, the industrial countries as a group should be running current account surpluses and lending on net to the developing world, not the other way around. If financial capital were to flow in this "natural" direction, savers in the industrial countries would potentially earn higher returns and enjoy increased diversification, and borrowers in the developing world would have the funds to make the capital investments needed to promote growth and higher living standards. (pp. 10-11)

UNDERSTANDING THE CURRENT ACCOUNT BALANCE

The trade balance and current account balance are distinct but overlapping measures. Like the trade balance, the current account reflects trade in services and goods (such as capital and consumer products, including agriculture), but the current account also includes net investment earnings to and from the rest of the world and is therefore a more complete measure of a nation's annual monetary inflows (borrowing) and outflows (lending) than the trade deficit alone.

The extent to which a country borrows or lends reflects the gap in that country between savings and investment. A current account deficit reveals that a country is borrowing from other countries to sustain investment at a level higher than would be possible given domestic savings. Countries that save more than they invest are net lenders and run a current account surplus. The reason countries save and invest at different levels is determined by a complex interaction of private behavior and public policies that are affected by interest rates, exchange rates, perceptions of risk, and income growth.

Until recently, observers typically pointed to low U.S. savings rates as the primary cause of rising current account deficits, a view supported by the fact that U.S. savings rates are low both by historical standards and relative to many other economies. While the U.S. gross national savings rate averaged

17.9 percent of GDP during the 1980s, and 16.9 percent during the 1990s, the savings rate has been under 14 percent since 2002.[1] This reflects both low public savings (budget deficits) and household savings rates that have declined from 7 percent of disposable household income in 1990 to less than 1 percent since 2004.[2] Lower savings rates are often attributed to "wealth effects" in which rising stock market values and appreciation in housing markets lead consumers to spend more of their disposable income.

In addition to lower savings in the U.S., other factors have contributed to increased U.S. current account deficits. One view is that the growing current account deficit is rooted largely in changing savings and investment behavior in other countries (Bernanke, 2005). According to this view, a series of financial crises in emerging economies since the mid-1990s and more recent oil price hikes created a "glut" of global savings. As a result, a number of emerging economies shifted from net borrowers internationally to net lenders beginning in the mid-1990s, as limited domestic investment opportunities caused savings to be channeled to the U.S. in search of additional investment opportunities or more secure returns. This development is reflected in the rising current account surpluses among oil exporters and Asia-Pacific countries that mirror the growing U.S. current account deficits since the mid-1990s.

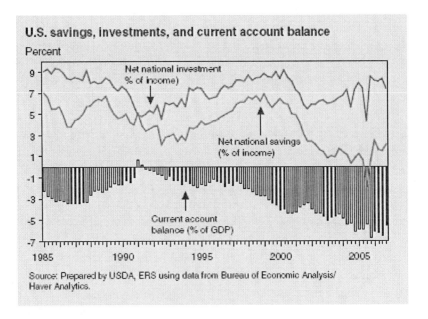

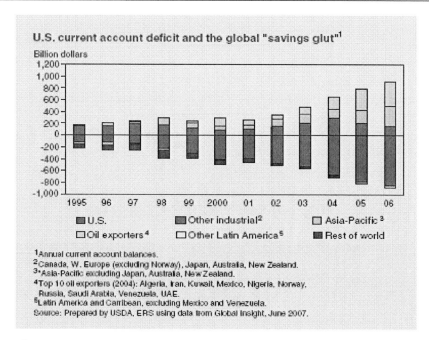

[1] Rising investment from 1991 to 2001 was also associated with generally increasing current account deficits, but a fall in investment following the 2001 recession was accompanied by even larger declines in savings, which led to continued growth of the current account deficits.

[2] The other major component of gross national savings is business savings. Note that the figure on the left refers to net, rather than gross, U.S. savings.

By extension, a return to "natural" conditions would imply that foreign savings eventually could be redirected back to investment opportunities in other emerging economies. As suggested by Bernanke, a desire to diversify savings out of the United States could also motivate a shift in assets from the United States to other developed or emerging economies.

Recent research also indicates that while few countries with large current account deficits have experienced sudden current account deficit "reversals,"[12] few countries have been able to maintain "persistent" and "high" current account deficits similar to the level currently experienced by the United States (Edwards, 2005). Edwards (2006) also notes that although the likelihood of large current account reversals is low for advanced countries with flexible exchange rates, the probability of a U.S. current account adjustment has increased significantly.[13] While the timing and magnitude of a potential U.S. current account "adjustment" is unclear, and perhaps not inevitable, even a relatively small or benign current account adjustment most likely would involve real exchange rate depreciation and higher interest rates (Corden,

2006). A weaker dollar would tend to raise foreign demand for U.S. exports of agricultural (and other) products because the price of U.S. goods would be cheaper in foreign currency terms. Similarly, the price of foreign agricultural (and other) products would increase for U.S. consumers, eventually dampening import growth (see, "The Role of Exchange Rates"). Higher interest rates in the United States would reinforce these tendencies if they were to result in reduced borrowing and spending on both imported and domestically produced agricultural products.[14]

THE ROLE OF EXCHANGE RATES

As a measure of the value of a country's currency, exchange rate changes affect the volume and value of a country's imports and exports. When the value of the U.S. dollar falls (depreciates) relative to another currency, for example, imports to the United States become more expensive in dollar terms even if the price in the foreign country remains constant in its own currency terms. Similarly, the price of U.S. goods and services become less expensive in foreign-currency terms even if the U.S. dollar price does not change. Thus, a depreciation of the dollar reduces the demand for, and value of, foreign goods in the United States, and increases the demand for U.S. goods abroad—raising net U.S. exports. A higher valued (appreciating) dollar will have the opposite effect. In practice, it can take some time before exchange rate changes affect trade flows or are reflected in prices paid by consumers (Carter and Pick, 1989).

Although there is a fairly strong historical relationship between exchange rates and the value of U.S. agricultural exports, the relationship is not as strong for agricultural imports. This has been especially true since 2002, when a weakening U.S. dollar corresponded with a rapid rise of imports.[1] While U.S. agricultural exports have grown fairly rapidly since the dollar began declining—rising by 26 percent ($13.7 billion) between FY 2002 and FY 2006—the value of U.S. agricultural imports has grown by 59 percent ($24 billion).

Some economists have suggested that one reason the overall U.S. trade balance continues to deteriorate is that the dollar has not depreciated sufficiently, in part due to the intervention of foreign governments in exchange markets (Bivens, 2004). Evidence does indicate that a number of countries accounting for a substantial share of U.S. bilateral trade—particularly in East

Asia—manage their currencies to support exports.[2] Nevertheless, the fact that the U.S. supplier trade-weighted exchange rate index has depreciated by nearly 20 percent between 2001 and 2005 indicates that these exchange rate rigidities, by themselves, are not responsible for the inability to stem the rise of U.S. imports.[3]

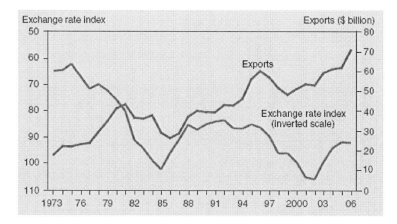

Sources: Imports: Bureau of the Census; exchange rates: USDA, ERS exchange rate data set, real trade-weighted exchange rate (U.S. suppliers, agricultural trade), www.ers.usda.gov/data/exchangerates/.

U.S. agricultural exports and the trade-weighted exchange rate index with U.S. markets

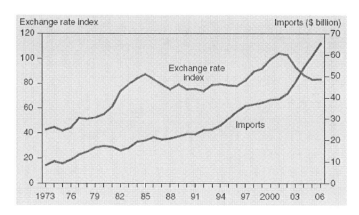

Sources: Imports: Bureau of the Census; exchange rates: USDA, ERS exchange rate data set, real trade-weighted exchange rate (U.S. suppliers, agricultural trade), www.ers.usda.gov/data/exchangerates/.

U.S. agricultural imports and the trade-weighted exchange rate index with U.S. suppliers

The long lag between the dollar depreciation since 2001 and a slowdown of imports reflects the price-inelastic (weakly responsive) U.S. consumer demand for imported agricultural products, perhaps caused by "wealth effects" discussed previously and/or limited pass-through of exchange rate changes to retail prices.[4] The general pattern reinforces the point that although the direction of the trade balance typically does track exchange rate movements—albeit with some delay—the overall level of the trade balance also reflects other factors affecting demand, such as consumer preferences, income growth, and savings and investment decisions in the United States and abroad.

[1] The real trade-weighted exchange rate indices in the figures are inflation-adjusted indices that measure changes in the value of the dollar against the currencies of U.S. agricultural export markets ("U.S. markets") and import suppliers ("U.S. suppliers"), respectively. The indices are weighted by the value of agricultural exports to countries using that currency (U.S. markets) and by the value of imports from U.S. suppliers. For information on how these indices are calculated, see www.ers.usda.gov/data/exchangerates/.

[2] Bivens (2004), for example, shows that the real trade-weighted exchange rate index with "major" U.S. trading partners accounting for about 55 percent of U.S. trade—such as the EU, Japan, Canada, and Australia—declined nearly 40 percent between January 2002 and December 2004. An index of "other trading partners" accounting for the rest of U.S. trade— countries such as Mexico, China, Korea, and Taiwan—indicated that the dollar weakened by less than 1 percent during the same time period.

[3] Currency rigidities may also explain the lack of U.S. agricultural export growth to some markets, such as Taiwan and Malaysia. However, China, with a fixed and widely perceived undervalued exchange rate, has been one of the fastest growing markets for U.S. agricultural exports and now ranks as the fourth largest U.S. agricultural export market.

[4] A study by Campa and Goldberg (2002) found that pass-through rates are significantly less for the U.S. than for other industrialized (OECD) countries, with as little as 40 percent of exchange rate movements passed through to U.S. import prices in the long run. Another study by Marazzi et al. (2005) also finds some evidence of a decline in pass-through rates over time for the food and beverage sector, particularly when compared with rates in the late 1980s.

OVERVIEW OF MODELING APPROACHES

Projecting and explaining historical shifts for U.S. and global trade requires taking into account numerous drivers of structural changes, such as global population growth, demographics, capital stocks, labor force, and income- related changes on consumption patterns, as well as macroeconomic variables, such as exchange rates, interest rates, savings, and investment. Because no single empirical model is capable of capturing all of these factors and their interactions, we employ two independent models to examine growth and macroeconomic influences separately.

Because global growth and macroeconomic factors involve an economy-wide perspective, we employ computable general equilibrium (CGE) models to simulate growth effects and macroeconomic change on agricultural trade. Such models are typically employed to gain broad insights on multiple economic interactions that would not be captured easily in other types of models. Capturing global economic interactions is important when major markets are growing at different rates. Countries are linked by international trade and capital flows, so that one country's economic growth affects that of its trading partners. Modeling these linkages provides more breadth and richness to economic analysis. However, a valid critique of this methodological approach is the highly aggregate structure used in such models. Some loss in detail of important features of actual food markets, such as product attributes, supply response, market structures, and consumer behavior, is one limitation of this approach (see appendix B for a fuller explanation of the models used in this analysis). However, the loss of detail is less critical when the analysis focuses on broader issues, as this study does, such as the effects of global growth on aggregate U.S. agricultural trade.

Modeling Global Growth Impacts

To evaluate the impacts of global economic growth and population changes on U.S. exports and imports, we employ the GTAP (Global Trade Analysis Project) model.[15] In this approach, world trade is simulated by exogenous shocks of historical and projected real GDP, capital, labor force, total factor productivity, and population changes.[16] The historical influence of these variables on trade is measured by conducting a "backcast" (backward forecast) to 1990. Backcasting allows us to compare the model's simulated growth projections of historical trade with actual historical changes in trade, and to assess the relative importance of economic growth for explaining historical trade growth. Using projections of economic growth with the same variables, the model simulates global trade forward to 2016. To underscore some key findings, our discussion of results focuses on the changing levels of U.S. exports to aggregated groups of "high-income" and "faster growing" economies.

Modeling Macroeconomic Impacts

Impacts of potential changes in foreign demand for U.S. financial assets on the U.S. economy and agricultural trade are examined using a single country model known as USAGE (United States Applied General Equilibrium). USAGE is a dynamic, computable general equilibrium model of the U.S. economy based on the theoretical structure of the Australian-based CGE model known as MONASH, which has been applied widely in forecasting and policy analysis.[17] In this study, we use an aggregate version of the full U.S. model consisting of 40 aggregated sectors, with agriculture comprising two industries: primary agriculture (crops and livestock) and food manufacturing. We focus on two hypothetical scenarios centered around a basic macroeconomic shock—changes in foreign investor demand ("confidence") for U.S. financial assets[18]—and trace out the effects of resulting exchange rate, interest rate, and other macroeconomic changes on domestic consumption and agricultural trade. The effects are measured as year-to-year deviations from a baseline projection, with the year 2002 as the starting point.[19] Two macroeconomic scenarios are considered:

- Scenario 1 simulates the effects of increased foreign demand for U.S. financial assets beginning in 2002 and represents enhanced confidence in the U.S. economy relative to foreign opportunities. This scenario is used to illustrate how increased foreign demand for U.S. financial assets feeds through the U.S. economy, affecting interest rates, exchange rates, consumption, and aggregate imports and exports. We introduce the shock in 2002 as a historical shock emulating effects of dollar appreciation on trade. The scenario is not meant to precisely reproduce actual historical developments. Instead, the scenario broadly simulates macroeconomic developments similar to those that led to the dollar's appreciation beginning in the mid-1990s and demonstrates how a single shock produces lasting trade effects.
- Scenario 2 is a shock capturing the effects of reduced foreign demand (confidence) for U.S. financial assets. This scenario reflects potential changes caused by improved investment opportunities abroad or concerns about the sustainability of the U.S. current account deficit that requires increased returns on U.S. assets. The shock is implemented in the same year. The purpose of this analysis is to illustrate a plausible outcome stemming from a change in foreign

investor behavior, not a predicted outcome. As stated previously, we can trace out the impacts on aggregate U.S. trade, as well as agricultural trade, by targeting a change in foreign demand for U.S. assets that produces a 20-percent depreciation of the dollar.

Model Results: Global Growth Effects on U.S. Trade

The analysis of global growth influences using the GTAP model illustrates three main points. First, the historical pattern of U.S. agricultural exports is broadly consistent with the simulated effects of global economic growth and population change. Although actual U.S. exports fluctuated considerably, the general pattern of modest growth, but with a shifting direction of exports to emerging markets, is corroborated. Second, consistent with model results, U.S. export growth has begun to accelerate since 2001, although the rapid growth of trade with individual markets, such as Mexico and Canada, cannot be attributed to economic growth factors alone.[20] If global growth continues, exports also can be expected to continue to grow at a faster pace during 2006-16 than during the 1990s due to the shift in U.S. and global exports toward the emerging markets. Lastly, the pace of U.S. imports was far higher than would be explained by U.S. economic growth and population change alone, indicating that other factors are responsible for the recent growth of U.S. imports.

The backcasting exercise demonstrates that historical changes in trade deriving from actual global growth are consistent with U.S. export growth patterns at the aggregate level. Between 1990 and 2001 (the GTAP model's base year), the projected effect of global growth and population change on U.S. export growth was a 2.6-percent annual growth rate, slightly higher than actual average export growth of 2.2 percent (table 2). Despite the surge (and subsequent decline) of actual U.S. exports in the mid-1990s, the actual pattern of modest growth for the entire period could have been anticipated because the slow-growing high-income markets initially accounted for the majority of U.S. exports (52 percent in 1990).[21] Over the same period, simulated annual export growth to high-income markets was 1.5 percent (1.7 percent actual), compared with projected growth of 4.6 percent to fast- growing emerging markets (5.1 percent actual).

Even though per capita income grew more in absolute terms (but not in percentage terms) in high-income markets than in faster growing emerging economies during the 1990-2001 period, food consumption and import demand in high-income countries slowed because the share of income spent on food was lower in these countries and continued to decline.[22] Diminished population growth in high-income markets also slowed growth in consumption and demand. U.S. exports to emerging economies grew more than twice as fast as exports to high-income countries, but the impact on overall export growth was moderated by the relatively low base from which exports to the rapidly growing markets started: 30 percent of the market for U.S. exports in 1990. The simulated historical trade pattern suggests that the slowing of U.S. agricultural exports was consistent with ongoing global structural shifts.

Although the broad pattern of simulated and actual U.S. export growth to the aggregated market groups was similar, the difference between simulated exports and actual export growth rates varied in individual markets. Trade agreements, the strength or weakness of different currencies, and unpredictable market developments for particular commodities affect how U.S. trade flows have evolved in particular markets. The GTAP model in this exercise did not account for these factors. For example, U.S. export growth to NAFTA partners is underprojected, and exports to "other" high-income countries (excluding Canada) are overprojected. Growth effects generated a 3.3-percent annual increase in U.S. exports to Mexico from 1990-2001, while actual exports to Mexico grew 9.3 percent annually. Similarly, actual U.S. exports to Canada during the same period grew about three times faster than predicted. These differences reflect the relative importance of NAFTA trade liberalization and the regional integration of the North American market during the time period. U.S. exports to China also grew much greater than projected during 2001-06, due partly to the general fostering of trade related to China's accession to the World Trade Organization (WTO) in 2001.

Conversely, U.S. exports to emerging markets other than Mexico and China failed to grow as much as projected. This was largely the result of devaluation of the foreign currencies affecting Southeast Asia and South Korea. As U.S. agricultural goods became more expensive for these markets, exports fell. Policy and other trade impediments also reduced export demand in other high-income markets, such as the EU and Japan, where U.S. exports were lower than the level consistent with population and economic growth changes alone. U.S. agricultural exports to "other high-income" markets (excluding Canada) would have increased by 1.1 percent annually from 1990 to 2001 due to economic growth effects, but exports actually declined 1.7 percent per year on average—an outcome attributable to policy-induced effects, such as the lack of market access in Japan, the effects of the EU's Common Agricultural Policy, and, possibly, demographic factors, such as the lower caloric needs of an aging population. These results underscore the important intervening effects of trade and domestic policies that are not explicitly considered in this model.

A second key finding is that, although future GDP and population growth are projected to slow in most countries—including the faster growing economies—more rapid growth of U.S. agricultural exports can be anticipated in the future due to the increasing share of U.S. exports flowing to countries with the highest growth rates. These effects are already apparent in recent export trends. For instance, U.S. export growth during 2001-06 averaged 5.3 percent annually, primarily due to accelerating growth in the key leading growth markets of China and Mexico. U.S. exports to these two countries surpassed the levels that were projected based on economic and population growth rates. Differences most likely stem from the effects of China's accession to the WTO in 2001 and ongoing trade liberalization with Mexico. U.S. export growth to other fast-growing emerging markets has been subdued relative to anticipated levels given the economic growth and population changes in these areas. Lack of market access in such countries as South Korea and Southeast Asia is a factor that continues to restrain U.S. agricultural exports.

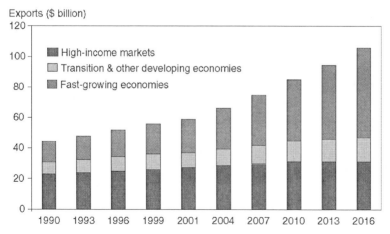

Note: High-income markets include Japan, Western Europe, Canada, and Oceania. Fast-growing economies include other East Asian countries, Southeast Asia, South Asia, Mexico, and Central America.
Source: USDA, ERS, GTAP model simulation, version 6.2 database.

Figure 6. Simulated global growth influences on U.S. agricultural exports

Table 2. Actual and predicted U.S. agricultural trade changes from global economic growth

Exports	Annual change, 1990-2001 Simulated	Annual change, 1990-2001 Actual	Annual change, 2001-06 Simulated	Annual change, 2001-06 Actual	Annual change, 2006-16 Simulated
Percent					
Exports					
Fast-growing emerging markets	4.6	5.1	6.9	12.1	6.6
China	7.8	8.9	12.1	27.7	10.1
Mexico	3.3	9.3	5.0	7.3	6.6
Other	4.6	2.8	6.5	3.3	5.6
High-income markets	1.5	1.7	1.5	2.4	0.1
Canada	2.3	7.6	2.5	7.1	1.9
Other high-income	1.1	-1.7	1.1	-0.2	-0.7
Other developing and transition	2.5	-1.6	3.8	5.1	2.2
Total exports	2.6	2.2	4.1	5.3	3.7
Total imports	2.0	5.0	1.8	10.3	1.6

Note: Predicted effects are simulated in the absence of all policy or exchange rate effects.
Source: USDA, ERS using GTAP model version 6.2.

GTAP model projections indicate that U.S. exports are projected to grow 3.7 percent annually during the 2006-16, compared with 2.2 percent actual growth during 1990-2001. The future growth is projected to come almost entirely from the emerging markets (figure 6). By 2016, the rapidly growing economies are projected to account for 56 percent of U.S. exports, up from 37 percent in 2001 and 30 percent in 1990. The share of U.S. exports going to high-income markets drops from 46 percent in 2001 to a projected 29 percent in 2016.

In contrast to the general results for U.S. exports, the rapid pace of U.S. agricultural imports in recent years cannot be attributed to the effects of economic growth and population change in the United States. Actual U.S. import growth dwarfed the level projected by the effects of U.S. economic growth and population. This is true for both the historical 1990-2001 period and the recent 2001-06 period. U.S. imports during 1990-2001 grew 5 percent annually, compared with simulated growth of 2 percent. During 2001-06, U.S. imports rose 10.3 percent annually, similar to import levels in some of the fastest growing emerging markets and much faster than the projected level of 1.8 percent. Other forces, such as shifts in preferences for food, regional market integration of the NAFTA countries, and high rates of consumption spending by U.S. households, contributed to import growth. Supported by wealth effects and other macroeconomic conditions discussed earlier, the high per capita income level of U.S. consumers has made U.S. food and beverage imports less sensitive to price fluctuations from exchange rates. In addition, the affluent and diverse population of the United States appears to demand greater product variety than do populations of other high-income countries.[23]

Model Results: The Impact of Macroeconomic Shocks on U.S. Trade

Macroeconomic influences are captured in the interaction between changing foreign demand for U.S. financial assets and various macroeconomic indicators, including exchange rates, interest rates, and consumption. The simulations illustrate how increased foreign demand for U.S. financial assets is linked to U.S. consumption growth, a stronger dollar, and increased net imports, whereas reduced foreign demand is likely to result in a weaker dollar, reduced consumption growth, and rising net exports. A key insight from the results is recognizing the role household spending on foreign goods has played in fostering aggregate consumption growth. This spending takes place mainly because of the willingness of foreigners to loan and invest their savings in the United States, which elevates the dollar at the expense of U.S. exports. The past growth of merchandise imports and current account deficits may set the stage for further macroeconomic adjustment in the future.

In scenario 1 (enhanced confidence), the required rate of return by foreign investors on U.S. assets in 2002 falls, triggering an initial dollar appreciation of 20 percent. This effect cuts total merchandise (agricultural and nonagricultural) exports on average by 8 percent per year during the ensuing period and increases real household expenditures (figure 7). The heightened attractiveness of the U.S. market for foreign investors depicted in scenario 1 thus drags down total U.S. exports, even as trade and domestic markets adjust over time, restoring the exchange rate closer to the original level. U.S. total foreign liabilities in the form of existing debt would continue to grow because the level of foreign debt in the U.S. has increased and must be serviced. This situation is sustainable as long as the U.S. economy continues to grow with sustained productivity providing the wherewithal to service foreign debt. The simulation scenario results reinforce the analytical conclusions presented earlier on macroeconomic forces that have been realized in the form of mounting U.S. trade and current account deficits.

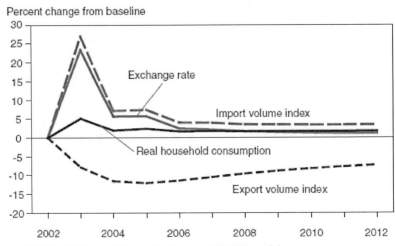

Source: USDA, ERS simulation with dynamic USAGE model.

Figure 7. Macroeconomic effects of a simulated increase of foreign demand for U.S. financial assets (2002)

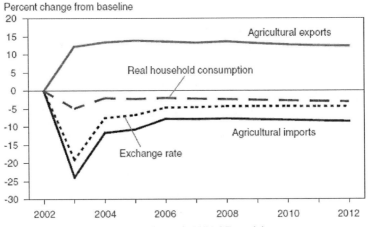

Source: USDA, ERS simulation with dynamic USAGE model.

Figure 8. Macroeconomic and agricultural trade effects on U.S economy of a simulated decline of foreign confidence

Scenario 2 depicts a sudden decline of confidence in U.S financial assets by foreign investors and further explores the consequences for U.S. agricultural trade. While a sudden decline in confidence—as modeled here—is plausible, the event could take place gradually, or not at all. The effect is the opposite of the influence of the enhanced confidence scenario (scenario 1), with the dollar initially depreciating and agricultural export volume increasing by about 13 percent (figure 8).[24] When the price of foreign goods increases relative to the price of U.S. exports, it results in a terms-of-trade loss, thereby reducing real household consumption. In addition, foreign capital that previously lowered borrowing costs now becomes rationed, further curbing consumption growth.

Depreciation of the dollar is not the only reason for reduced import growth, but rather acts in conjunction with the simulated effects of lower overall consumption growth. Recent experience demonstrates that without a slowdown in consumption growth, exchange rate depreciation may not by itself reduce imports. Between 2001 and 2006, for example, U.S. agricultural imports from the EU rose rapidly despite a substantial depreciation of the dollar against the euro. This effect may stem from the inelastic price demand of U.S. consumers for many imported specialty products—that is, a given price change induces a relatively small change in quantity demanded. Furthermore, the continued strength of U.S. consumption led to an increased quantity of imports, which translated into an even larger increase in value terms due to the weaker dollar. In actual market conditions, the extent to which exchange rate changes affect U.S. agricultural exports and imports also depends on which foreign markets experience the greatest exchange rate changes, lags in purchasing behavior by importers and exporters (the "J-curve effect"), and the degree to which exchange rates are passed through to buyers.[25] Nonagricultural import growth has already begun to diminish since 2006 as a result of weakening U.S. demand for foreign goods and higher import prices.[26]

CONCLUSION

A history of uneven growth for U.S. agricultural exports raises the question of whether the U.S. will face a slowdown in foreign demand for U.S. agricultural exports after several years of strong expansion. In the past, wide fluctuations in U.S. agricultural trade arose from unsteady import demand from maturing markets. Decreases in demand in these countries were attributed to slow growth in consumption and the effects of policy factors simulating local production. With growth in population and GDP potentially slowing in emerging foreign markets, reduced growth in U.S. agricultural exports in the next decade is a plausible outcome. Findings indicate, however, that while U.S. export growth was adversely affected by slower growth in developed countries during the 1990s, the shifting direction of U.S. exports to faster growing emerging markets could continue to support the renewed strength of U.S. export growth. A continuation of this global structural shift could provide a foundation for ongoing export growth in the coming decade because the lower per capita incomes and more youthful age structures of emerging markets are associated with rising food demand. As a result, U.S. and world agricultural trade has greater potential for growth in the coming decade than in the previous decade.

Fluctuations in U.S. agricultural trade also stem from macroeconomic influences driven by wealth effects and domestic and foreign savings patterns that affect the dollar and consumer spending on foreign goods. In the absence of a change in foreign investor preferences for U.S. financial assets, it is possible that U.S. consumption and the value of the dollar will remain relatively stable, leading to continued robust growth of agricultural imports. However, if foreign investors diversify their asset holdings away from U.S. assets, rising foreign demand for U.S. products associated with income growth would be reinforced by dollar depreciation and lower priced U.S. goods for foreign consumers. Analysis of potential changes to macroeconomic conditions demonstrates that curtailed growth of the U.S. current account deficit would be associated with slower U.S. household spending, a weakening dollar, and improved prospects for net exports.

Although many other factors will influence agricultural trade going forward, structural shifts in foreign economic growth and macroeconomic influences both point to more sustained growth of U.S. agricultural exports in the future and a potential downturn for import growth from its current pace.

APPENDIX A. PUTTING THE TRADE BALANCE IN PERSPECTIVE

As discussed previously in this chapter, our analysis and scenario results suggest that global growth trends and macroeconomic fluctuations may sustain the renewed growth of U.S. agricultural exports and potentially subdue import growth in the coming decade. Although the food sector encompasses a broad and diverse set of interests, this path is likely to be perceived as beneficial for the agricultural sector, especially given the attention to the narrowing of the agricultural trade balance in recent years.[27]

Most economists are quick to remind others that the trade balance is not a meaningful measure of consumer well-being (welfare), and that reaping the gains from trade necessarily requires that, over time, net exports in some sectors are offset by net imports in others. In addition, several specific points about U.S. agricultural trade illustrate that, even for an individual sector, the trade balance at any given time is not necessarily the best barometer of a sector's financial condition or relative competitiveness. First, although exports are an important component of agricultural demand, the recent decline of the trade surplus has not corresponded with reduced incomes at the farm level. U.S. agricultural exports and farm incomes have been at or near record levels in recent years. Instead, the agricultural trade surplus has declined largely because a strong economy and robust consumer spending have raised import growth to unprecedented levels, particularly for processed and consumer-ready products. Second, although imported foods constitute a growing share of U.S. food consumption, U.S. "dependence" on imported agricultural products remains low—about 14 percent of domestic food and beverage consumption by volume—compared with that of many other countries. Third, while the U.S. faces increasing competition, both domestically and abroad for some agricultural products, the sector as a whole continues to have a strong advantage in trade compared with most other sectors of the economy.

Farm Sector Revenues Strong Despite Lower Trade Surplus

A country's trade or current account balance cannot by itself be taken as a primary indicator of its economy's health or the well-being of its consumers. In fact, rising trade deficits, or diminishing surpluses, are often associated with periods of strong economic growth, as rising incomes allow consumers to purchase both more imports and domestically produced items. Many economists also observe that there is nothing inherently wrong with a trade deficit, or inherently desirable about a surplus. Countries trade with one another because it allows them to consume products that are either different, not available, or less expensive than domestic goods. Trade provides the further benefit of encouraging specialization, which allows countries to make products (goods or services) more efficiently, thus lowering consumer prices and raising real incomes.

Changing trade patterns—such as rising overall deficits or increased competition for a particular industry or sector—do, however, have economic consequences requiring adjustments by both producers of tradable goods and consumers. Sectoral trade balance developments are also often closely observed as an indicator of the strength of demand and, hence, returns to the labor, land, and capital resources used to produce outputs in that sector. For example, a declining market share for a particular industry or sector implies declining employment and lower returns (wages, profits) to those associated with that sector. A persistent deficit also means that current consumption is being financed through borrowing from abroad. Eventually, increased exports and/or lower imports, and thus lower consumption (or sale of U.S. assets), will be required to repay that borrowing.

In the case of agriculture, though, the recent dip in the sector's trade balance has not coincided with general financial stress in the farm sector. In contrast to the mid-1980s—when farm incomes suffered and exports declined—net farm incomes have been comparatively strong in recent years, bolstered in part by government payments to farm producers. farm incomes surpassed $60 billion for the first time in 2003 and exceeded that level in each of the ensuing 4 years. Revenues from farm commodities have also reached record levels in recent years.[28] Current farm wealth and debt-toequity ratios are also favorable compared with those of previous years. This partly reflects the fact that U.S. agricultural exports rose during the past several years and reached a record $78 billion in FY 2007. In many ways, change in the agricultural sector's trade balance reflects the strong overall domestic spending—and its underlying causes—which has affected trade in all sectors of the economy (app. figure 1).

Imported Share of U.S. Food Consumption Remains Low

Some observers have expressed concerns that a lower agricultural trade surplus, and fast-rising imports in particular, indicates increasing dependence on foreign sources of food. Agricultural imports do constitute a growing share of U.S consumption, but the share remains a relatively small proportion of overall food expenditures. Furthermore, many imported products (e.g., tropical goods, seasonal fruit and vegetables) do not compete directly with U.S. grown goods, are nonfood products (e.g., tobacco), or are processed "luxury" products, such as wine or malt beverages. Several additional points should be kept in mind:

- In 2005, the United States imported $40 billion of processed food—about two-thirds of total agricultural imports. A decade ago, U.S. processed food imports were less than half as much. Although Americans' appetite for imported processed food and beverages is rapidly rising—largely due to a more diverse population, a wider range of food preferences and choices, and higher disposable incomes—the share of processed food imports in domestic consumption remains small at 5 percent, based on wholesale value. Similarly, the import share of unprocessed food in domestic consumption, including fresh fruits and vegetables, is 10 percent. These relatively low import shares do not reflect high dependence on imported food.
- Close to 90 percent of U.S. agricultural imports of $59 billion in calendar year 2005 was for food use. Of these food imports, about a third are either not grown or produced in the United States or are more cheaply supplied from foreign sources, including bananas, coffee, cocoa, olive oil, pineapples, avocados, mangos, and cashew nuts. The strongest import growth has been among horticultural products. Many fresh fruit and vegetables are seasonal and can only be supplied from other countries during the winter months. The remaining 10 percent of U.S. agricultural imports are nonfood goods, such as tobacco, rubber, flowers, hides and skins, and nursery products.
- Not only are U.S. affiliates of foreign food companies helping supply the U.S. domestic market with locally produced processed food and beverages, but they contribute significantly to U.S. agricultural export earnings. The U.S. processed food and beverage industries generated $553 billion in sales in 2003, of which 13 percent, or $73 billion, was sold by foreign-owned food manufacturers operating in the United States. Of the $30 billion of U.S. processed food exports in 2003, $8.3 billion, or 27 percent, were shipped by these foreign-owned companies. Without these companies, U.S. dependence on imported food would be higher and U.S. agricultural exports would be smaller.

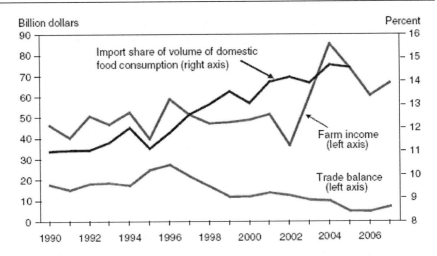

Sources: Trade balance (1990-2006 fiscal year): Bureau of the Census; 2007 data (forecast) from "Outlook for U.S. Agricultural Trade, August 2007, http://usda.mannlib.cornell.edu/MannUsda/viewDocumentInfo.do?documentID=1 196; farm income:(www.ers.usda.gov/briefing/farmincome/data/va_t1.htm); import share: compiled by USDA, ERS, updated from Amber Waves, February 2004, www.ers.usda.gov/amberwaves/february04/features/ ustradebalance.htm

Appendix figure 1. Farm income strengthened despite rising food imports

U.S. Maintains a Comparative Advantage in Agriculture

In the shorter term, exchange rate movements and other factors that influence relative prices certainly affect the competitiveness of U.S. agriculture, but longer term underlying patterns of trade—the composition of goods and services that a country exports and imports—continue to reflect the factors determining a country's comparative advantage in production and trade, such as the relative abundance and quality of land, labor, and capital (Dohlman, Osborne, and Lohmar, 2003). Despite changes in the agricultural trade balance, indicators of comparative advantage suggest that the United States continues to retain an advantage in production and trade of agricultural products, particularly land-based bulk commodities.

One indicator of the relative competitiveness of U.S. agriculture—and the importance of exports to the sector—is the exported share of the volume of agricultural production. In value terms, the share of U.S. agricultural output that is exported is roughly double the proportion exported by the rest of the economy. By volume, exports accounted for over 20 percent of U.S. agricultural output during 2003-05.[29] Productivity gains have allowed the United States to simultaneously produce, consume, and export more agricultural products. The share of agriculture in U.S. GDP has declined steadily over the years, but the value (as measured by gross cash income) of agricultural production has continued to climb.

Another measure of the comparative advantage of agriculture in U.S. trade is the revealed comparative advantage (RCA) index. The RCA index measures the extent to which an exporting country captures world market share in a particular sector relative to its export share for all traded goods (Regmi et al., 2005). An RCA greater (less) than one signifies a comparative advantage (disadvantage) for the particular item. According to Regmi et al. (2005), U.S. agricultural products as a whole, and "land-based foods" (e.g., bulk commodities) in particular, have maintained their comparative advantage in trade. In contrast to the very strong comparative advantage of U.S. land-based foods, U.S. manufactured foods did not have a comparative advantage during 1989-2001. However, RCAs for manufactured products rose in the latter part of this period, indicating increasing competitiveness.[30]

APPENDIX B. THE GTAP AND USAGE MODELS

Simulating Global Growth Effects Using the GTAP Model

The standard GTAP model is a static model used commonly for policy analysis. However, the model can be used for specialized purposes as is done in this report. Trade policies remain constant, and the effects of growth alone and its implications for trade are assessed. In the model, economic growth has both a supply-side and a demand-side component. In order for the growth to take place, factors of production must increase. In the standard model for trade policy analysis, factors of production are fixed. In the growth scenarios conducted in this report, these become exogenous shocks (determined outside the model) and are targeted to specific points in time both in the past and in the future (app. figure 2). To maintain equilibrium conditions for supply and demand, income accrues to households as payments to the primary factors, labor and capital. The model determines economic income generated from growth in factors of production. Income is spent by the household on goods and services and taxes, and used for savings. To assess how global economic growth affects U.S. trade, we adopt an approach similar to that employed by Coyle et al. (1998) and Gehlhar and Coyle (2001) using the GTAP framework. For simulating historical growth effects, we use a general approach, termed "backcasting" (or backward forecasting), which takes as exogenous the population, labor force, capital stock, and GDP variables. We use the model to determine how U.S. agricultural trade was influenced by growth with all trading partners in the past and the implications of economic growth on changes in the directions of trade in the future. To make global projections, we use projected growth in real GDP, capital, labor (skilled and unskilled), and population. Capital stock projections are estimated consistently from projections of gross domestic investment. Capital stock and labor estimates for individual countries are based on estimates prepared by the Center for Global Trade Analysis as a baseline prepared for a dynamic version of the GTAP model (Ianchovichina and McDougall, 2002). Total factor productivity is endogenized while targeting prespecified GDP levels. This is done at the economy- wide level. Ideally, we would prefer to adopt sector-specific rates of productivity. This is particularly critical for agricultural productivity growth.[31]

The standard model has undergone a number of improvements since the earliest version of standard GTAP modeling. These improvements all have some bearing on the ability of the model to reproduce historical trade patterns. Some of the most critical features with implications for agricultural trade are demand-side specification and trade elasticities in the model.[32] Modifications of the demand side include calibrating to own price and income elasticity targets of nine consumption goods that are derived from estimated parameters. In doing so, expenditure and price responsiveness can vary considerably from high-income countries to low-income countries for different goods.

Trade pattern shifts are simulated from global trade models often governed heavily by trade elasticities known as Armington elasticities. Previous parameters in the standard GTAP model were based on outdated and highly aggregated estimates that restricted the ability to reproduce historical trade shifts. As a result, price changes for home and foreign goods could change by unrealistic magnitudes. Better methodologies for generating estimates based on Hummels (1999) have become available for more appropriate estimates of the elasticity of substitution among imports from competing sources. Other estimates, including those by Harrigan (1995) and Trefler and Lai (1999), also support higher elasticities of substitution parameters than the original estimates used in the GTAP model.

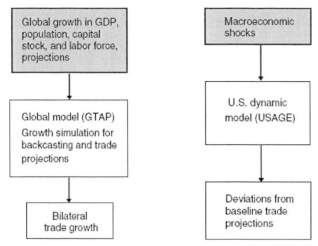

Source: Prepared by USDA, ERS.

Appendix Figure 2. Schematic of modeling approaches

Measuring Macroeconomic Influences with the USAGE Model

Approaches to examining the influence of macroeconomic variables on agricultural trade often focus on exchange rate movements and their long- and short-term effects (see Carter and Pick, 1989; Mattson and Koo, 2005). Macroeconomic influences, however, can involve a multitude of factors beyond exchange rate price effects. Our analysis examines a broader question of how U.S. agricultural trade might be affected by macroeconomic factors as a result of shifting foreign demand for U.S. assets, which, in turn, can affect domestic consumption of goods in the United States and the rest of the world. The framework we employ is a dynamic computable general equilibrium model of the United States known as MONASH-USA, developed by Dixon and Rimmer (2002). This type of model has been widely applied in forecasting, policy analysis, estimation of technology trends, and analysis of historical events for the Australian economy. The USAGE model has many distinguishing features, including the explicit treatment of international financial flows. Although the model can be run with 500 industries, the dynamic version of the model used here is aggregated to 40 sectors. We use the aggregated version of the USAGE model. Our primary interest is obtaining estimates of the impact of macroeconomic influences on U.S. trade, which does not require full industry detail. The aggregated version retains the main theoretical features of full-scale Monash-style models. The dynamic aspects of the USAGE model described in Dixon and Rimmer (2002) include physical capital accumulation and rate-of-return-sensitive investment; foreign debt accumulation and the balance of payments; public debt accumulation and the public sector deficit; and dynamic adjustment of wage rates in response to gaps between the demand for and supply of labor. The model has explicit treatment of net foreign liabilities, where the current account deficit includes payments for servicing foreign-owned assets, and payments on foreign debt, where all foreign liabilities are assumed to be debt repayable in U.S. currency.

As described by Dixon and Rimmer (2002), the model can be run with four basic closures: historical closure, decomposition closure, forecast closure, and policy closures.[33] The model is capable of producing estimates of changes in technological change and consumer preferences, explanations of historical developments, forecasts for industries, and deviations from forecast paths that would be caused by proposed policies and by other shocks, such as macroeconomic shocks.

REFERENCES

Bernanke, Ben. (2005). "The Global Saving Glut and the U.S. Current Account Deficit," Remarks by Governor Ben S. Bernanke, Homer Jones Lecture, St. Louis, MO, April 14, *http://www.federalreserve.gov/ boarddocs*/speeches/2005/ 20050414/default.htm.

Bivens, L. J. (2004). *Debt and the Dollar: The United States Damages Future Living Standards by Borrowing Itself into a Deceptively Deep Hole*, Economic Policy Institute (EPI) Issue Brief No. 203, December 14.

Campa, J. M. & Goldberg, L. (2002). "*Exchange Rate Pass-Through into Import Prices: A Macro or Micro Phenomenon?*" NBER Working Paper Series, Working Paper 8934, May.

Carter, C. A. & Daniel, H. (1989). Pick. "The J-Curve Effect and the U.S. Agricultural Trade Balance," *American Journal of Agricultural Economics, Vol. 71*, No. 3.

Corden, W. (2006). Max. "*Those Current Account Imbalances: A Sceptical View*," Melbourne Institute Working Paper Series, No. 13/06, June.

Coyle, W., Gehlhar, M. J., Hertel, T. W., Wang, Zhi, & Yu Wusheng. (1998). "Understanding the Determinants of Structural Change in World Food

Markets," *American Journal of Agricultural Economics, 80(5)*, 1051-1061.
Dixon, P. B. & Rimmer, M. T. (2002). "Dynamic General Equilibrium Modeling for Forecasting and Policy: A Practical Guide and Documentation of Monash," *Contributions to Economic Analysis, 256*, North-Holland Publishing Company, Amsterdam, xiv+338.
Dohlman, E., Osborne, S. & Lohmar, B. (2003). "Dynamics of Agricultural Competitiveness: Policy Lessons From Abroad," *Amber Waves*, Vol. *1*, Issue 2, April.
Edwards, Sebastian. *"Is the U.S. Current Account Deficit Sustainable? And If Not, How Costly Is Adjustment Likely To Be?"* NBER Working Paper Series, Working Paper 11541, August 2005.
Edwards, Sebastian. *"The U.S. Current Account Deficit: Gradual Correction or Abrupt Adjustment?"* NBER Working Paper Series, Working Paper 12154, March 2006.
Federal Reserve Bank of San Francisco. *"What If Foreign Governments Diversified Their Reserves?"* FRBSF Economic Letter 2005-17, July 29, 2005, http://www.frbsf.org/publications/economics 17.html.
Food and Agricultural Organization of the United Nations (FAO). Statistics, 2006, http://faostat.fao.org/.
Gale, F. & Huang, K. (2007). *Demand for Food Quantity and Quality in China*, Economic Research Report No. 32, U.S. Department of Agriculture,
Economic Research Service, January 2007, www.ers.usda.gov/publications/err32/err32.pdf.
Gehlhar M. & Coyle, W. (2001). "Global Food Consumption and Impacts on Trade Patterns," in *Changing Structure of Global Food Consumption and Trade*. Agriculture and Trade Report No. WRS-01-1, U.S. Department of Agriculture, Economic Research Service, May.
Global Insight. http://www.globalinsight.com/EconomicFinancialData/.
Harrigan, J. (1995). "The Volume of Trade in Differentiated Products: Theory and Evidence," *Review of Economics and Statistics, 77*(22),283-293, May.
Harrison, W. J. & Pearson, K. R. (1996). "Computing Solutions for Large General Equilibrium Models Using GEMPACK," *Computational Economics*, Vol. *9*, 83-127.
Haver Analytics. http://www.haver.com/ Hertel, T.W. (ed.). *Global Trade Analysis: Modeling and Applications*, New York: Cambridge University Press, 1997.
Hummels, D. (1999). *"Towards a Geography of Trade Costs,"* GTAP

Working Paper No. 17, Center for Global Trade Analysis, Purdue University, West Lafayette, IN.

Ianchovichina, E. & McDougall, R. (2002). *"Theoretical Structure of Dynamic GTAP,"* GTAP Technical Paper No. 17, Purdue University, , http://www.agecon.purdue.edu/gtap/GTAP-Dyn.

Lee, Jong-Wha, W. McKibbin, & Park, Y. C. (2004). *"Transpacific Trade Imbalances: Causes and Cures,"* CAMA Working Paper 14/2004, Centre for Applied Macroeconomic Analysis, The Australian National University, November 2004, http://cama.anu.edu.au.

Ludena, C. E., Hertel, T. W., Preckel, P., Foster, K. & Nin Pratt, A. (2006). *"Productivity Growth and Convergence in Crop, Ruminant, Non-Ruminant Production: Measurement and Forecasts,"* Working Paper No. 35, Center for Global Trade Analysis, *https://www.gtap. agecon.purdue. edu*/resources/working_papers .asp.

Mann, Catherine. (1999). *Is the U.S. Trade Deficit Sustainable?* Institute for International Economics, September.

Marazzi, M., Sheets, N. & Vigfusson, R. et al. (2005). *Exchange Rate Pass-Through to U.S. Import Prices: Some New Evidence.* International Finance Discussion Papers, No. 833, Board of Governors of the Federal Reserve System, April.

Marris, Stephen. (1987). Deficits and the Dollar: The World Economy at Risk, Institute for International Economics, Policy Analyses in International Economics 14, Updated Edition.

Mattson, J. & Koo, W. (2005). *Characteristics of the Declining U.S. Agricultural Trade Surplus*, Agribusiness & Applied Economics Report No. 572, Center for Agricultural Policy and Trade Studies, November.

McKibbin, W. J. (2005). *"Global Demographic Change and Japanese Macroeconomic Performance: Results for Japan,"* Brooking Discussion Papers in International Economics, Working Paper 3.04, Lowy Institute for International Policy.

McKibbin, W. J. (2006). *"The Global Macroeconomic Consequences of a Demographic Transition,"* Working Paper 6, Center for Applied Macroeconomic Analysis, http://cama.anu.edu.au.

Mellor, John. (1982). "Third World Development: Food, Employment, and Growth Interactions," *American Journal of Agricultural Economics*, Vol. *64*, 304- 311, May.

Obstfeld, M. & Rogoff, K. (2004). *"The Unsustainable U.S. Current Account Position Revisited,"* NBER Working Paper 10869, October.

Organisation for Economic Co-operation and Development (OECD).

Economic Survey of the United States, 2004, OECD Policy Brief, April 2004.

Regmi, Anita (ed.). *Changing Structure of Global Food Consumption and Trade*, Agriculture and Trade Report No. WRS-01-1, U.S. Department of Agriculture, Economic Research Service, May 2001, www.ers.usda.gov/publications/wrs0 11/.

Regmi, A., Gehlhar, M., Wainio, J., Vollrath, T., Johnston, P. & Kuthuria. N. (2005). *Market Access for High-Value Foods*, Agricultural Economic Report No. 840, U.S. Department of Agriculture, Economic Research Service, February, www.ers.usda.gov/publications/aer840/ aer840.pdf.

Reimer J. & Hertel, T. W. (2003). *International Cross-Section Estimates of Demand for Use in the GTAP Model*, GTAP Technical Paper No. 23.

Roe T., Shane, M. & Vo, D. H. (1986). *Price Responsiveness of World Grain Markets: The Influence of Government Intervention on Import Price Elasticity*, Technical Bulletin No. 1720, U.S. Department of Agriculture, Economic Research Service.

Schnepf, Randall, E. Dohlman, & Bolling, C. (2001). *Agriculture in Brazil and Argentina: Developments and Prospects for Major Field Crops*, Agriculture and Trade Report No. WRS-01-3, U.S. Department of Agriculture, Economic Research Service, November.

Seale J., Regmi, A. & Bernstein, J. (2003). *International Evidence on Food Consumption Patterns*, Technical Bulletin No. 1904, U.S. Department of Agriculture, Economic Research Service.

Shane, Mathew, Terry Roe, and Agapi Somwaru. "*Exchange Rates, Foreign Income, and U.S. Agriculture*," Economic Development Center Staff Paper. University of Minnesota, July 2006.

Shi, Q. & Tyers, R. (2005). "*Global Demographic Change and Economic Performance: Applications of an Augmented GTAP-Dynamic*," Working Papers in Economics and Econometrics No. 450, Australian National University.

TD Economics. *Will U.S. Treasuries Pay a Price for Record Foreign Indebtedness?* Special Report, April 2006, http://www.td.com/economicsbc0406_treas.pdf.

Trefler, D. & Lai, H. (1999). *Gains From Trade: Standard Errors With the CUS Monopolistic Competition Model*, University of Toronto.

Tyers, Rod, (2005). "*Aging and Slower Population Growth: Effects on Global Economic Performance*," Presented at the "Experts' Meeting on Long Term Scenarios for Asia's Growth and Trade," Asian Development Bank, November.

United Nations Population Division. *"World Population Prospects, The 2002 Revision: Population Database-Assumptions Underlying the Results of the 2002 Revision of World Population Prospects,"* 2006, http://esa.un.org/unpp/assumptions.html.

U.S. Department of Agriculture (USDA), Economic Research Service (ERS). Agricultural Exchange Rate Data Set, www.ers.usda.gov/data/exchangerates/.

U.S. Department of Agriculture (USDA). *Outlook for Agricultural Trade*, AES-54, August 31, 2007, http://www.fas.usda.gov/cmp/outlook /2007/May07/outlook-0507.asp.

U.S. Department of Agriculture (USDA). *USDA Agricultural Projections to 2016*, OCE-2007- 1, February 2007, http://www.ers.usda.gov/publications/ oce07 1/oce2007 1.pdf.

U.S. Department of Agriculture (USDA). *USDA Agricultural Baseline Projections to 2015*, OCE-2006-1, February 2006, www.ers.usda.gov/publications/oce06 1/.

U.S. Department of Agriculture (USDA). *USDA Agricultural Baseline Projections to 2011*, Staff Report WAOB-2002- 1, February 2002, www.ers.usda.gov/publications/waob021/waob20021.pdf.

U.S. Department of Agriculture (USDA). *Long-Term Agricultural Projections to 2005*, Interagency Agricultural Projections Committee, Staff Report WAOB-96-01, February 1996.

U.S. Department of Commerce, Bureau of the Census. http://www.census.gov/foreign-trade.

The World Bank. World Development Indicators, 2006, http://web.

End Notes

[1] Specifically, we examine how U.S. trade is influenced by U.S. and foreign savings, investment, and consumption behavior and the mechanisms (e.g., exchange rates and interest rates) that transmit these to prices and demand.

[2] At the time, USDA (USDA, 1996) projected that the value of U.S. agricultural exports would reach $78.8 billion in 2005, up from $54.2 billion in 1995, citing developing countries as a major source of export demand growth. Actual exports were valued at $62.5 billion in 2005.

[3] In nominal terms. The value for 2008 is projected.

[4] Income growth has not always translated into food import growth. China, for example, only recently became a major market for the United States but only for a few basic commodities. A reason for the lack of high- value food product trade with China is that much of the country's newly formed wealth remains highly concentrated among its wealthiest consumers (Gale and Huang, 2007). Japan, the EU, and NAFTA partners still account for about 70 percent of U.S. processed food exports. A shift toward a rising share of processed

products in U.S. agricultural exports subsided with slowing exports to Japan and the EU and limited growth to non-NAFTA trading partners.

[5] In the results section of this report, we distinguish broadly between groups of countries at three levels of economic development: high-income markets, transition and other developing economies, and fast-growing (emerging) economies. High-income markets consist primarily of such countries as Japan and Canada and the regions of Western Europe and Oceania. Transition and other developing economies refer primarily to the former Soviet Union, Eastern Europe, and Africa. Fast-growing (emerging) economies refer to East Asian countries (other than Japan), Southeast Asia, South Asia, Mexico, and Central America.

[6] Another dimension of global agriculture is the ongoing change in the composition of trade. In the past two decades, imports of processed products by high-income countries have been growing faster than global trade in bulk commodities, so the composition of global agricultural trade has shifted from bulk toward high-value products. Thus, while the U.S. has generally maintained its global market share in bulk commodities, its total share of global agricultural trade has drifted downward as the composition has shifted to high-value products. U.S. high-value product exports are also notably more concentrated in far fewer markets (such as Canada, Japan, and the EU) than are bulk exports, so limited U.S. export growth was also associated with the lack of representation in faster growing markets.

[7] As measured by an index of real trade-weighted exchange rates (with U.S. markets), the value of the dollar declined from an index value of nearly 106 in 2002 to less than 92 in 2006 (as of September 2006). By this measure, the value of the dollar remains higher than in all but 11 years dating back to 1970 (see USDA, ERS).

[8] Note that the U.S. Department of Commerce "Food, Feeds, and Beverages" category shown in figure 5 is not directly comparable with the USDA definition of agriculture. BEA, 2004 data from "latest news release" 7/13/2005, tables, exhibit 13, *www.bea.gov/bea/di/home/ trade* 1997 data from www.census.gov/for- eign-trade/Press-Release/97_press_releases/ Final_Revis ions_1997/exh12.txt

[9] Financial crises in Mexico (1994), East Asia (1997), Russia (1998), Brazil (1999), and Argentina (2002) dampened investment demand in these countries and led to an increased flow of savings to external investment opportunities. Following the 1997-98 Asian financial crisis, for example, the region (excluding Japan, Australia, and New Zealand) moved from a small current account deficit to consistent surpluses—largely reflecting a decline in investment rather than a change in savings. Domestic investment in seven East Asian economies fell from a 1996 average of 35 percent of GDP to less than 24 percent during 1998- 2002 (Lee, McKibben, and Park, 2004). Increased earnings from oil- exporting countries also found their way into global financial markets due to limited domestic investment opportunities. Although the "oil-exporting" countries had current account surpluses throughout most of the past decade, their collective surpluses have grown from an average of $52 billion annually during 1995-2002 to $212 billion during 2003-05.

[10] By the end of 2005, foreign investors owned over one-fourth of all U.S. treasury notes, and more than half (about $2.2 trillion) of privately held treasuries (TD Economics, 2006). In 2004, the amount of privately held U.S. treasuries was roughly the same as foreign central bank reserves, mostly dollar denominated reserves held by Asian countries (Obstfeld and Rogoff, 2004).

[11] Korea, Japan, and China, among the top holders of dollar-denominated foreign currency reserves, all have indicated the possibility of diversifying their foreign exchange reserves in recent years. For a brief discussion of the implications of such a change, see Federal Reserve Bank of San Francisco, 2005.

[12] Defined by Edwards (2005) as either a reduction in the current account deficit of at least 4 percent of GDP in a 1-year period (and an accumulated reduction of at least 5 percent over 3 years), or 2 percent of GDP in 1 year (and an accumulated reduction of at least 5 percent over 3 years).

[13] Specifically, Edwards estimates that the probability of a U.S. current account reversal has grown from 1.7 percent in 1999 to 14.9 percent in 2006.

[14] For more information on how the U.S. economy would adjust to a reduced flow of foreign savings and the key equilibrating market mechanisms (exchange rates, interest rates, and economic activity), see Marris (1987), particularly chapter 4.

[15] See https://www.gtap.agecon.purdue.edu/

[16] This was the framework employed by Coyle et al. (1998) and Gehlhar and Coyle (2001) to perform a growth simulation with the GTAP model.

[17] See http://www.monash.edu.au/ policy/mon-usa.htm

[18] Changes in demand are represented by a change in the required rate of return by foreign investors. A gain of confidence lowers the required rate of return by foreign investors, while reduced confidence raises the required rate of return.

[19] The USAGE model's base year is updatable to any recent year depending on availability of both macroeconomic and factors of production data, including capital and labor statistics for the U.S. economy.

[20] The phaseout of tariffs on trade in NAFTA and the influence of foreign direct investment and arm's length transactions all contributed to the rapid growth in agricultural trade

[21] High-income markets include Japan, Western Europe, Canada, and Oceania. Faster growing economies include other East Asian countries, Southeast Asia, South Asia, Mexico, and other Central American countries.

[22] This is a feature of the model's demand specification that is supported by econometric evidence.

[23] Recent trade statistics for U.S. food and beverage imports indicate a widening mix of country sources. For example, the United States now imports wine from more than 40 countries. The ethnic makeup of the U.S. population has broadened food preferences and increased demand for foreign-made products.

[24] A number of factors affect exchange rates and impacts on import and export volumes, including government intervention (see Roe, Shane, and Vo, 2006).

[25] The J-curve effect refers to an initial deterioration of the trade balance following a depreciation of the exchange rate due to inelastic demand for imported products in the shorter term, and the time it takes domestic producers to increase output of the import-competing good.

[26] See http://www.census.gov/foreign-trade for current trade in U.S. total merchandise imports and exports.

[27] Interests would vary based on commodity produced, size, location, position in the processing or retail chain, and other factors.

[28] For information on the USDA, ERS 2007 farm income and cost forecast, see www.ers.usda.gov/ briefing/farmincome/nationalestimates.htm

[29] See "indicators" in the latest issue of Amber Waves, available at *www.ers.usda.gov/ amberwaves/allissues/*

[30] Regmi et al. (2005), pp. 23-26.

[31] A methodology developed recently by Ludena et al. (2006) provides better treatment of commodity- specific productivity rates within primary agriculture and processed food. This method could be used to generate productivity projections for specific agricultural sectors. Ideally, projections for agriculture should include productivity using this methodology.

[32] See Reimer and Hertel (2003) for elaboration for cross-section estimates of demand for use in the GTAP model.

[33] A closure is a specified set of variables that become endogenous or exogenous for a given simulation. Closure depends on the objective of the model simulation.

CHAPTER SOURCES

The following chapters have been previously published:

Chapter 1 – This is an edited, reformatted and augmented version of a Congressional

Chapter 2 – This Research Service publication, Report 98-253, dated March 15, 2010.is an edited, reformatted and augmented version of a United States Department of Agriculture publication, report FAU-124, dated April 2008.

Chapter 3 – This is an edited, reformatted and augmented version of a United States Department of Agriculture publication, Economic Research Report Number 46, dated September 2007.

INDEX

A

access, 44, 60, 84, 85
accounting, 74, 78, 80
adjustment, 62, 73, 74, 77, 87, 98
Africa, 17, 20, 103
age, 71, 72, 90
Agency for International Development, 41
aging population, 64, 71, 85
agricultural exports, vii, 1, 2, 8, 9, 11, 32, 34, 35, 36, 40, 43, 44, 45, 46, 47, 48, 49, 50, 51, 52, 53, 55, 56, 57, 60, 61, 62, 63, 64, 65, 66, 67, 68, 69, 71, 73, 78, 79, 80, 83, 84, 85, 89, 90, 91, 92, 93, 102, 103
agricultural sector, 2, 48, 69, 91, 92, 104
agriculture, vii, 59, 63, 69, 73, 75, 82, 92, 94, 95, 103, 104
annual rate, 2
appetite, 93
Argentina, 14, 17, 18, 21, 25, 69, 101, 103
Asia, 32, 33, 34, 35, 69, 70, 71, 76, 79, 84, 85, 101, 103, 104
asian countries, 85, 103, 104
assets, 62, 63, 65, 73, 74, 77, 82, 87, 88, 89, 90, 92, 97
authority, 40

B

balance of payments, 98
banks, 40
barriers, 44
base, 50, 56, 83, 84, 104
base year, 56, 83, 104
BEA, 48, 103
beef, 1, 6, 20, 40, 67
beer, vii, 1, 2, 29
benefits, 44
benign, 77
beverages, 73, 93
bonuses, 40
borrowers, 73, 75, 76
Brazil, 2, 13, 17, 18, 20, 21, 23, 27, 28, 31, 69, 101, 103
budget deficit, 76
Bureau of Labor Statistics, 51, 58
Burkina Faso, 19, 20
buyers, 89

C

Cameroon, 19, 20
capital accumulation, 98
capital flows, 81
capital inflow, 65, 73, 74

Caribbean, 28
cash, 40, 95
cattle, 41
census, 45, 47, 48, 52, 53, 64, 68, 71, 74, 79, 94, 102
Central African Republic, 19, 20
central bank, 73, 103
Chad, 19, 20
cheese, 20, 41
China, 1, 2, 11, 12, 15, 17, 22, 23, 34, 35, 61, 67, 69, 71, 72, 80, 84, 85, 86, 99, 102, 103
closure, 98, 104
cocoa, 29, 53, 93
coffee, 29, 53, 93
Colombia, 2, 32
commodity, 8, 29, 37, 41, 45, 46, 49, 50, 51, 55, 104
comparative advantage, 69, 94, 95
competition, 44, 91, 92
competitiveness, 91, 94, 95
competitors, 13, 69
composition, 45, 46, 55, 94, 103
computer, 51
concessional terms, 41
consensus, 62
consumer demand, 44, 80
consumer goods, 73
consumers, 37, 44, 49, 50, 53, 61, 64, 66, 71, 72, 76, 78, 87, 89, 90, 91, 92, 102
consumption, 49, 50, 62, 63, 65, 66, 67, 72, 73, 80, 82, 83, 87, 89, 90, 91, 92, 93, 96, 97, 102
consumption patterns, 80
cost, 104
cotton, 1, 4, 8, 9, 13, 44, 69
crises, 73, 76, 103
crop, 4, 8, 69
crops, 6, 7, 49, 69, 82
currency, 73, 74, 78, 80, 98, 103
current account, viii, 59, 60, 62, 63, 72, 73, 74, 75, 76, 77, 82, 87, 88, 90, 91, 98, 103, 104

current account balance, 75, 91
current account deficit, viii, 59, 62, 63, 72, 73, 74, 75, 76, 77, 82, 87, 88, 90, 98, 103
current account surplus, 74, 75, 76, 103
customers, 46

D

data processing, 46, 53
data set, 79
database, 4, 7, 14, 15, 17, 18, 19, 21, 23, 24, 25, 27, 28, 85
decomposition, 98
deficit, 44, 62, 72, 73, 74, 75, 76, 77, 82, 90, 91, 92, 98, 103
demographic factors, 84
Department of Agriculture, vii, 1, 3, 4, 5, 6, 7, 8, 9, 10, 11, 12, 13, 14, 15, 16, 17, 18, 19, 20, 21, 22, 23, 24, 25, 26, 27, 28, 29, 30, 31, 32, 33, 34, 35, 36, 37, 99, 101, 102, 105
Department of Commerce, 48, 54, 58, 64, 68, 71, 74, 102, 103
depreciation, 65, 73, 74, 77, 78, 80, 83, 89, 90, 104
destination, viii, 11, 51, 59, 61
devaluation, 84
developed countries, 90
developing countries, 44, 69, 71, 73, 75, 102
direct investment, 104
direct payment, 37
disposable income, 76, 93
distribution, 46, 51, 52, 68
diversification, 73, 75
domestic economy, 49
domestic investment, 76, 96, 103
domestic markets, 87
Dominican Republic, 28, 29
donations, 41

Index

E

earnings, 62, 75, 93, 103
East Asia, 79, 85, 103, 104
Eastern Europe, 103
economic activity, vii, viii, 43, 46, 48, 49, 50, 51, 53, 56, 57, 59, 63, 69, 104
economic consequences, 92
economic development, 60, 63, 66, 67, 103
economic growth, 34, 60, 61, 62, 64, 65, 66, 67, 71, 81, 83, 84, 85, 86, 90, 91, 95
economic growth rate, 60
economic methodology, 54
economic reform, 41, 67
economic theory, 74
economics, 99, 101
economy, 44, 45, 48, 49, 50, 51, 53, 55, 67, 73, 81, 82, 88, 91, 92, 95, 96, 97
Egypt, 71
elaboration, 104
emerging markets, 40, 44, 61, 63, 64, 66, 68, 69, 71, 83, 84, 85, 86, 87, 90
employment, vii, 43, 44, 46, 49, 50, 51, 55, 56, 92
enlargement, 28
equilibrium, 81, 82, 95, 97
equity, 72
EU enlargement, 28
Europe, 69, 71, 75, 85, 103, 104
European Union (EU), 1, 2, 11, 12, 13, 14, 20, 21, 23, 24, 25, 27, 28, 29, 31, 32, 34, 38, 64, 66, 67, 71, 72, 80, 84, 89, 102, 103
evidence, 72, 80, 104
exchange rate, 60, 62, 65, 67, 72, 73, 75, 77, 78, 79, 80, 82, 86, 87, 89, 94, 97, 102, 103, 104
exercise, 83, 84
expenditures, 40, 70, 87, 92
export market, 11, 13, 27, 32, 80
exporter, 1, 13, 20, 27, 44
exporters, 20, 40, 69, 73, 76, 89

exports, vii, 1, 2, 6, 7, 8, 9, 11, 13, 20, 27, 28, 32, 33, 34, 35, 36, 37, 40, 43, 44, 45, 46, 47, 48, 49, 50, 51, 52, 53, 54, 55, 56, 57, 58, 59, 60, 61, 62, 63, 64, 65, 66, 67, 68, 69, 70, 71, 72, 73, 78, 79, 80, 81, 82, 83, 84, 85, 86, 87, 89, 90, 91, 92, 93, 蚀94, 102, 103, 104

F

farm income, 91, 92, 94, 104
farms, 46
fat, 40
field crops, 7
financial, 40, 46, 51, 53, 62, 65, 73, 74, 76, 82, 87, 88, 89, 90, 91, 92, 97, 103
financial capital, 74
financial condition, 91
financial crisis, 103
financial institutions, 40
financial market, 74, 103
fish, 49
fishing, 49
flour, 9, 41
flowers, 29, 93
fluctuations, 87, 89, 90
food, viii, 37, 41, 43, 44, 46, 48, 49, 51, 52, 53, 59, 60, 61, 63, 64, 66, 67, 68, 69, 70, 71, 73, 80, 81, 82, 83, 87, 90, 91, 92, 93, 94, 102, 104
food products, 64
force, 80, 81, 96
forecasting, 82, 96, 97
foreign direct investment, 104
foreign exchange, 103
foreign investment, 62
France, 71
free trade, 31
fruits, vii, 1, 2, 8, 9, 29, 93
funds, 75

G

global demand, 74
global economy, 2
global trade, vii, 43, 59, 68, 69, 80, 81, 96, 103
goods and services, 40, 53, 62, 78, 94, 95
government intervention, 104
government payments, 92
government policy, 2
government spending, 37
governments, 78
Gross Domestic Product (GDP), 34, 54, 62, 65, 66, 68, 69, 70, 72, 74, 76, 81, 85, 90, 95, 96, 103
growth, vii, 32, 33, 34, 35, 37, 44, 46, 59, 60, 61, 62, 63, 64, 65, 66, 67, 68, 69, 70, 71, 72, 73, 75, 77, 78, 80, 81, 83, 84, 85, 86, 87, 89, 90, 91, 93, 95, 102, 103, 104
growth factor, 62, 65, 83
growth rate, 60, 61, 69, 83, 84, 85

H

health, 91
history, 89
Hong Kong, 12
horticultural crops, 69
household income, 76
housing, 72, 76
human, 49

I

Iceland, 41
imbalances, 73
impacts, 45, 49, 50, 54, 62, 65, 68, 71, 81, 83, 104
import prices, 80, 89
imported products, 53, 92, 104
imports, vii, 1, 2, 29, 31, 43, 44, 49, 50, 53, 56, 57, 59, 60, 61, 62, 63, 64, 65, 67, 68, 69, 72, 78, 79, 80, 81, 82, 83, 86, 87, 89, 90, 91, 92, 93, 94, 96, 103, 104
improvements, 96
income, vii, viii, 34, 43, 44, 46, 47, 50, 53, 54, 55, 56, 58, 59, 60, 61, 63, 64, 66, 67, 68, 71, 72, 75, 76, 80, 81, 83, 84, 85, 86, 87, 90, 94, 95, 96, 103, 104
increased competition, 92
India, 13, 15, 18, 19, 69, 71, 72
indirect effect, 50
individuals, 60
Indonesia, 2, 32, 71
industrial sectors, 46
industries, 46, 48, 51, 55, 82, 93, 97, 98
industry, 48, 50, 55, 68, 92, 98
inferences, 66
inflation, 80
institutions, 73
integration, 68, 84, 87
interest rates, 62, 65, 72, 73, 75, 77, 80, 82, 87, 102, 104
international trade, 81
interrelatedness, 50
intervention, 78, 104
investment, 50, 62, 73, 75, 76, 77, 80, 82, 96, 98, 102, 103
investment opportunities, 75, 76, 77
investment rate, 73
investments, 73, 75
investors, 65, 73, 74, 87, 89, 90, 103, 104
ions, 103
issues, 81

J

Japan, 1, 11, 12, 34, 35, 38, 41, 60, 64, 66, 67, 69, 71, 72, 75, 80, 84, 85, 100, 102, 103, 104

K

Korea, 1, 11, 12, 38, 41, 80, 84, 85, 103

L

labor force, 80, 96
Latin America, 32, 33, 35, 36, 37, 69, 70, 71
lead, 68, 73, 76
lending, 62, 73, 74, 75
liberalization, 67, 68, 84, 85
livestock, 4, 6, 7, 29, 69, 82

M

macroeconomics, 60
mad cow disease, 1, 20
magnitude, 77
majority, 83
Malaysia, 80
management, 53
manufacturing, vii, 43, 46, 49, 51, 56, 57, 82
market access, 44, 60, 84, 85
market share, 13, 20, 27, 92, 95, 103
market structure, 81
marketing, 4, 13, 14, 15, 17, 29, 53
matrix, 54, 55, 56
mature economies, 61
meat, 20, 41
merchandise, 65, 87, 104
methodology, 45, 47, 48, 52, 53, 54, 104
Mexico, 1, 2, 11, 12, 28, 31, 32, 33, 35, 36, 37, 44, 61, 67, 69, 71, 72, 80, 83, 84, 85, 86, 103, 104
middle class, 71
modeling, 62, 65, 96, 97
models, 48, 62, 65, 81, 96, 98
modification, 56
multiplier, 49, 50, 53, 57
multiplier effect, 49

N

natural resources, 69
net exports, 50, 73, 87, 90, 91
net farm income, 92
net investment, 62, 75
New Zealand, 1, 2, 20, 21, 24, 25, 27, 32, 41, 103
North America, 2, 11, 44, 84
North American Free Trade Agreement, (NAFTA), 2, 11, 31, 32, 35, 36, 37, 44, 68, 84, 87, 102, 104
Norway, 41
nutrition, 41

O

Oceania, 85, 103, 104
oil, 8, 9, 41, 73, 76, 93, 103
oilseed, 8, 44, 49
olive oil, 93
opportunities, 44, 75, 76, 77, 82, 103
Organization for Economic Cooperation and Development, 2, 37, 39
output method, 45, 47, 48, 52, 53

P

Pacific, 69, 76
packaging, 51
Pakistan, 13, 15
Paraguay, 18
parity, 68
per capita income, 66, 71, 72, 83, 87, 90
policy, 2, 37, 63, 66, 67, 82, 84, 86, 90, 95, 97, 98, 104
population, 60, 61, 62, 64, 65, 66, 67, 68, 69, 71, 72, 80, 81, 83, 84, 85, 86, 90, 93, 96, 104
population growth, 61, 62, 65, 66, 67, 68, 69, 80, 84, 85

poultry, 7, 8, 20, 29, 41
price changes, 51, 96
price deflator, 56
price effect, 97
probability, 77, 104
producers, 37, 92, 104
product attributes, 81
productivity, 55, 56, 87, 96, 104
productivity growth, 96
productivity rates, 104
public debt, 98
public sector, 98
purchasing power, vii, 43, 44, 68
purchasing power parity, 68

Q

quotas, 40

R

rate of return, 87, 104
real income, 92
recession, 2, 77
recommendations, 60
reforms, 41, 67
regional integration, 84
relative prices, 94
requirements, 46, 51, 55
reserves, 73, 103
resources, 69, 92, 100
response, 81, 98
responsiveness, 96
retail, 80, 104
risk, 75
rubber, 29, 93
Russia, 12, 103

S

savings, 62, 65, 72, 73, 75, 76, 77, 80, 87, 90, 95, 102, 103, 104

savings rate, 65, 75
school, 41
services, 40, 46, 50, 51, 52, 53, 56, 57, 62, 73, 75, 78, 92, 94, 95
shock, 82
shores, 50
showing, 56
signals, 61
signs, vii, 59, 63
simulation, 85, 88, 104
simulations, viii, 59, 62, 65, 87
South Africa, 17
South America, 35, 36
South Asia, 34, 35, 85, 103, 104
South Korea, 1, 11, 12, 84, 85
Southeast Asia, 34, 35, 69, 84, 85, 103, 104
Soviet Union, 32, 33, 103
soybeans, vii, 1, 4, 8, 9, 13
specialization, 91
spending, 37, 65, 72, 73, 78, 87, 90, 91, 92
stakeholders, 61
statistics, 49, 104
storage, 40
stress, 92
structural changes, 80
structure, 45, 54, 71, 72, 81, 82
style, 98
subsidy, 40
substitution, 96
succession, 67
supplier, 1, 13, 20, 31, 41, 79
suppliers, 1, 2, 20, 79, 80
surplus, vii, 1, 2, 41, 44, 60, 63, 73, 75, 91, 92
sustainability, 73, 82
Switzerland, 41

T

Taiwan, 1, 11, 12, 20, 22, 23, 80
tariff, 2, 40, 41
taxes, 95

Index

taxpayers, 37
technological change, 98
technology, 97
Thailand, 13, 15
Third World, 100
tobacco, 8, 44, 92, 93
Togo, 19, 20
total factor productivity, 81
trade, vii, 1, 2, 9, 28, 29, 31, 35, 37, 41, 43, 44, 45, 46, 47, 48, 49, 50, 51, 52, 53, 54, 56, 58, 59, 60, 61, 62, 63, 64, 65, 66, 67, 68, 69, 71, 72, 73, 74, 75, 78, 79, 80, 81, 82, 83, 84, 85, 86, 87, 88, 89, 90, 91, 92, 94, 95, 96, 97, 102, 103, 104
trade agreement, 31, 44
trade benefits, 44
trade deficit, 44, 65, 75, 91
trade liberalization, 67, 68, 84, 85
trade policy, 63, 66, 67, 95
trading partner, 35, 44, 80, 81, 96, 103
transactions, 104
transport, 51
transportation, vii, 43, 46, 49, 51, 56, 57, 58
treatment, 97, 104
Turkey, 12, 41

U

U.S. Department of Commerce, 48, 54, 58, 64, 68, 71, 74, 102, 103
U.S. Department of Labor, 56, 58
U.S. economy, 43, 44, 45, 46, 49, 50, 53, 62, 65, 72, 74, 82, 87, 104
Ukraine, 14, 17, 25, 27
united, 1, 2, 4, 6, 7, 13, 14, 15, 17, 18, 19, 20, 21, 22, 23, 24, 25, 27, 28, 31, 32, 37, 39, 40, 41, 44, 49, 50, 54, 55, 58, 62, 67, 68, 69, 71, 72, 73, 74, 77, 78, 80, 82, 86, 87, 93, 94, 95, 97, 98, 99, 102, 104, 105
United States, 1, 2, 4, 6, 7, 13, 14, 15, 17, 18, 19, 20, 21, 22, 23, 24, 25, 27, 28, 31, 32, 37, 39, 40, 41, 44, 49, 50, 54, 55, 58, 62, 67, 68, 69, 71, 72, 73, 74, 77, 78, 80, 82, 86, 87, 93, 94, 95, 97, 98, 101, 102, 104, 105
USDA, 2, 3, 37, 40, 41, 45, 47, 48, 52, 53, 56, 58, 60, 61, 64, 65, 68, 70, 71, 72, 74, 79, 85, 86, 88, 94, 97, 102, 103, 104
USSR, 32
Uzbekistan, 13, 18, 19

V

valleys, 46
variables, 62, 65, 80, 81, 96, 97, 104
vector, 55, 56
vegetable oil, 41
vegetables, vii, 1, 2, 8, 9, 29, 92, 93
Vietnam, 13, 15, 71
volatility, 46

W

wage rate, 98
weakness, 84
wealth, 62, 65, 72, 76, 80, 87, 90, 92, 102
welfare, 91
well-being, 91
Western Europe, 75, 85, 103, 104
wholesale, 93
workforce, 51, 55, 57
World Bank, 72, 102
World Trade Organization (WTO), 2, 34, 40, 41, 84, 85

Y

young people, 71